3/24

Suffering Eyes

A Chronicle of Awakening

Franceen Neufeld

Edited and with an afterword by
Calvin Neufeld

Purposeful
Publishing

All proceeds from *Suffering Eyes* are donated to farm animal sanctuary. For more information or to contribute to the rescue, visit:

www.sufferingeyes.com

Purposeful Publishing House
57 Foster Street, Box 2012
Perth, Ontario, Canada
K7H 1R9
www.purposefulpublishinghouse.com

ISBN 978-0-9920658-0-5

Printed in Canada on 100% recycled paper.

This book is dedicated to my mother

Marie Georgette Michelle Fauteux
December 12, 1923 ~ August 12, 2012

whose compassion embraced all living creatures.

Acknowledgement

It is with deepest gratitude that I acknowledge the contributions of my son, Calvin Neufeld, towards the creation of this book. I am indebted beyond words to the stamina, vision, instinct, generosity, creativity, wisdom, honesty, understanding, incisiveness, kindness, companionship, expertise, and above all – love – that my son put into editing and publishing *Suffering Eyes*. This book is the legacy I want to leave to the world, for the alleviation of suffering and the cultivation of kindness. So the thanks that I owe to Calvin is for the greatest gift I could ever receive – the gift of my life being effective for goodness and mercy. And for happiness.

Contents

Kindness is more important than wisdom,
and the recognition of this is the beginning of wisdom.

Theodore Isaac Rubin

It is better to love a little than to understand everything.

George MacDonald

A disciple asks the rebbe, "Why does Torah tell us to 'place these words *upon* your hearts'? Why does it not tell us to place these holy words *in* our hearts?" The rebbe answers: "It is because as we are, our hearts are closed, and we cannot place the holy words in our hearts. So we place them on top of our hearts. And there they stay until, one day, the heart breaks and the words fall in."

Hasidic tale

Apologia

the bird

One Thanksgiving dinner, someone called it "the bird" one too many times, and with that, my Mom stopped eating meat. For years – decades, really – we humoured her. Mused over her sentimentalism. Recounted her cuteness in entertaining stories about her sensationally soft-headed excesses. Dismissed her choices as irrelevant to us. And most of all, laughed.

Remember the time she performed mouth-to-mouth resuscitation on the drowned dragonfly? Remember when she fed rats on the picnic table outside her dining room window so they wouldn't come inside the house? Remember how she put extra food and water out for the mice in her house when she went on holiday, so they wouldn't go hungry while she was away? And how when she caught those mice in a live trap and brought them outside, she was careful not to take them too far for fear they might get lost?

Remember how every time she pulled up a weed, she said "I'm sorry."

Why has it taken me so long to understand my mother's wisdom? To see how far ahead of us she was?

How is it that I, animal lover as I have always considered myself to be, was able – year after year – to give Thanks by reaching inside a slaughtered being, without giving so much as one thought to what "its" life (and death) had meant to "it"? As I pulled out all those delicate organs, I didn't let my mind go back to the time when each one of these tiny miracles played its deft part in mediating life for this majesty of a bird. Until that one awful moment when some cold hand ripped apart this creature's whole little world, held up its limp and broken body, and stuffed it with its own mangled bits and pieces, like some unspeakable desecration.

We laughed at my mother. How could we?

Looking Back

my mother's heart

My childhood is a dense fog, with little mountain tops poking out here and there in the landscape of my memory. Far away in the distance, one of those peaks rises high and strong, and yet vague in everything but the sound of it. The sound is a scream, my mother's scream. My child's eyes do not understand, but the shattering of that scream resounds in my world still.

A mother bird preparing for her little ones, carefully crafting a cradle for them, has hung herself from the eaves of the house. I hear my mother's heart screaming, and my own chest feels it still, tightens around my heart that can't bear the horror of it any more than my mother's could.

In those days it was my mother's distress that bewildered me. Now it is my own. What can I possibly do with this much agony for the world of misery surrounding me, if the tragic suffering of a little bird – or even of a helpless insect – is capable of making me pound my fists into my brain to make it stop seeing, thinking, feeling? How can I rouse myself from mindlessly rocking my spirit back and forth and going nowhere?

I venture forward because I have no other choice. These words that I write become my steps. I force them from me one at a time, no longer caring what awaits me around the next corner. I choose not to heed the fear – it can't be worse than being eaten away from the inside out.

Suffering surrounds us, lies at our feet. I thought I could hide but I can't. What is left? I choose friendship. I choose to be *with*. Let my own skin be wounded, let the blood of our separate worlds be mingled. Let grievances be anointed with tears and bandaged by kindness.

I choose my mother's heart, the heart that had no talent for hiding from the suffering of the innocents. That is her greatest legacy to me, and the treasure I hope to leave to my own children.

blinders

Not right to be unkind. Can anything be simpler, or more foundational, than this?

I remember the shock and horror I felt as a child, when I saw my classmates deliberately seek out creeping lives to snuff out with the soles of their shoes. *Why why why* would they do that? I still don't understand.

And yet I myself was not immune to that dark side of childhood innocence, the inability to experience the world through the eyes of another. I loved finding baby toads in the field near my home. It was fun to gather them. Of course I didn't hurt them, but when a friend asked me to mind her snake for her, I caught those baby toads and released them into the snake's cage. I think I watched. The horror of what I was capable of doing stays with me yet. The horror, mostly, that I don't remember feeling conflicted about it.

And here is the dilemma: I know that the law of "tooth and claw" is natural, that the imperatives of hunger and self-protection can preclude mercy, shut the door against it. Life has its necessities, we kill when we have to. Who would advocate allowing lice to take up residence in one's hair? Sometimes we need emotional blinders to protect our hearts from what we are required to do.

But to kill when other options are available?

Why keep blinders over our eyes beyond the sphere of necessity? Why kill our fellow travellers in this world when we don't need to?

Why kill mercy in our hearts?

limping

Guilt. My actions harming another, irreparably. What do we do with that? How do we possibly go on when we cannot take back an action, cannot go back in time to the instant before we did what we did? My first memory of that breed of guilt involved such a little life. But it was all the life that tiny creature was ever to have, and I had irreversibly altered and diminished it, perhaps condemning it to a long and slow death. I don't know, because as soon as the awful wave of realization flooded over me, my clumsy capturing hands released their helpless prisoner. And the little grasshopper, missing one beautiful leg, disappeared into the grass.

I don't think I revealed to anyone the damage that was done to my spirit that day. From that moment on, I was condemned to limping along with one foot still barefoot with childhood, the other plastered over with the weight of adolescent cares.

My heart had meant no wrong. But benign or malignant, the result had been the same – I had snapped off the fruit from the tree of living things, and it could never be reattached. No way to go back to a time before awareness that I exist at the expense of others.

Yesterday I mowed our unkempt square of spring grass. How many unseen lives did I trample and slice and sacrifice? Thankfully I noticed the plump frog in time and nudged him to safety.

So what is the answer? Steel the heart to the inevitability of harm? Trample with impunity? Or let my own limp forever remind me of that first known creature whose life was harmed by my existence in the world. Remember, and step as lightly as possible.

I closed the book

I closed the book. But not before it had drawn me in and held me just long enough to end my childhood. I took the veil in that moment and hid myself away, not from the eyes of the world, but from the pain of it. But a veil is flimsy protection and only serves to blur the grief, smearing the starkness of its black and red into the dirty grey of hopelessness.

A book of fictional stories, but with a dagger of truth at the heart of each one. The faithful dog, with blood dripping from its mouth, shot to death just before the enraged father realizes that the dog had protected the child, not harmed it. The goat, chained to a stake as live bait, helpless, alone and terrified in the darkness, unable to escape the coming violence. Story after agonizing story. I have forgotten the title of that book, and I have not thought of those tales in a very long time. But they have become the colour of my world and I don't know how to change that until the world itself grows brighter.

I wonder at my presence in this world. I am implicated in its ugliness every time I sit on leather chairs and each time I take medications whose safety was wrung out of pathetic creatures broken for me. I am implicated every time I keep silence, choosing artificial human harmony over the profound peace possible only through the pursuit of justice for all living beings.

It all feels one to me now. Suffering eyes have but one call on my heart – the urgent imperative to remove the veil and face the truth.

the others

My mind is searching out its less familiar hallways and I find a door I have never thought to open. I know what I will find if I enter that room. And what it will do to me.

She was a lovely dog. The people who rescued Pandy already had a dog and didn't want another, but they thought she was so cute that they couldn't let her be drowned. So they scooped her up and carried her away from her helpless mother and doomed siblings, and they found us to care for her.

The others. It is the others who are behind that door. They will not go one more day without someone shedding tears over how life betrayed them.

Did they live for hours? For days? For weeks? Not for longer. How many were they? Were they baby boys or baby girls? No one to weep for them. No one to rage for them. No one to imagine what it was like for them when their baby lungs filled to bursting with the unwelcome of their unwanted lives. Perhaps no one – until this moment – to cast even a brief or passing thought their way.

Pandy, did they have your lovely dark eyes? Your playful faithfulness? Your big-bad-wolf smile? Did they look like little panda bears too? As you and I grew up together, did you retain any faint memories of those little ones who had tumbled about with you during those early morning hours of your life? If they had lived and you had met again, would some deep memory have recognized the blood connection you shared?

And your mother. Pandy, that is the one place I cannot go. But I must – go that one step further into that dark room. Did she see them being torn from her side? Did she try to hold on to them?

That's as far as I can go.

blue skies

Complicated and conflicted, my memories.

Birds kept to amuse us, sad and lonely, talking to mirrors, hearing distant twitters of sunlit cousins, stretching cramped wings in response, instinctively readying themselves for the miracle they were never to know. Except for the one who escaped, high and beyond, seizing moments of soaring joy at the cost of slow starvation or inevitable cold, or surrender to some new confinement. I was never to know.

Fish circling, suffocating, ignored on some shelf. Rodents curled in smelly cage corners, alone and forgotten.

These were the pets we loved.

My mind lingers with special tenderness on our succession of beloved dogs. Faithful guardians, tender souls, they deserved so much better than the leftover morsels of our family's patience and understanding. I did not love them as a mother would, and that has become a great grief to my heart.

And then there was my bullfrog. He at least was free. When I went as a child to my grandmother's cottage, I would stretch out my arms to him and he would swim to me and climb onto my hand. I had taught him to trust me. And then one day he didn't come. I heard that my grandmother's neighbours used to eat the legs of frogs like mine. Had I taught him to trust people, only to unwittingly betray him to others of my own kind? I was never to know.

My childhood is peppered with memories of horses. They infused my life with happiness. I talked with them, stroked their great strong necks, touched my cheek to their exquisite noses, fed them carrots and apples and sugar cubes, climbed onto their backs and exhilarated at the speed and power beneath me. But now. Now I think of the lonely dark prisons where they wait on the whims of people like me, and where blue skies and mercy and green grass are charities doled out to suit our convenience.

Standing stark and separate in my memory is the university farm we visited regularly with our own children. The farm was modern and clean, a model of efficient productivity. We stroked cats, were licked by cows, and watched as chains dragged a calf from his mother's womb. A place where we saw but did not see. Holes cut into the sides of cows for the purposes of science. Pigs living in sterile cleanliness, never seeing the light of day. Motherhood coerced and hours-old babies wrenched from each new mother's side to be confined in bewildered solitude. Why did we not wonder why? How is it that year after year we could visit this place for our family's enjoyment, and the horror of it not register in our consciousness? Until that one day as we watched the new mechanical floor passing beneath the cows to clean up their mess, tripping them as it passed beneath them, first one way then the other, over and over again, no rest for the weary ones struggling to keep their footing. We were all sad that day. We never returned. And I tried to forget.

Now as my grandchildren embark on their own animal-loving lives, what am I to tell them? How can I ensure that my late and painful awakening will serve to enrich their joy rather than diminish it?

All I know is that if I were living my own childhood over again, or the childhood of my children, blue skies and mercy and green grass would not be optional.

we lied

We lied to the lamb. Not with words – no words passed between us about what was coming. But with gentle hands caressing and tender arms embracing, we assured this helpless baby that we were on his side. I wonder where his mother was, how she felt when her sweet little child was taken away. But now we stood in for her, feeding her little one with a bottle, guarding, protecting, nurturing. Helpless and alone, without his mother, he now depended upon us, trusted us. We embraced the little orphan, cared for him tenderly, and then slit his throat.

We lied to you, little helpless one. The real message was between the lines, between our teeth as our forked tongues lusted to steal from you.

This is the heart of our darkness. The treachery of everything we do to all these beings. Always it is the same – we lie and we lie and we steal and we steal. As if it doesn't matter what that does to them or to our own souls.

There are times when my own species shames me until I can no longer bear it. I cannot bear that I belong to this faithless race, so well rehearsed in our treachery that we no longer see through our own act. We fool ourselves as much as we fool our prey, so that one and all they follow us meekly to the bloodied hell we have prepared for them.

We steal their milk, we steal their eggs, we steal their babies. And then, when they have nothing left to give us, we steal their life, and watch it drip slowly from their eyes.

And in our own eyes we see ourselves as just and honourable and compassionate all the same.

mercy

I remember when everything I thought I knew fell out from under me in one split second of time. A road-wounded bird, my plea for help, my husband's foot descending to crush it. The rest of that day passed for me through a distant lens. It was as if I had been banished to some remote place that had no meaning, no bearings. My husband kept calling to me to come back. Explaining, regretting, calling to me.

And all the while, it was he who had mercy.

Justice, mercy, humility – these are the virtues that call to me. Three cords pulling on me. What is the place of balance between them, the harmony of their tension? How do I travel through this world "acting justly, loving mercy, walking humbly"? Pretty words, but so often in conflict with each other, like arrows pointing in opposing directions, urging, tugging, keeping me wandering in circles.

I think the words themselves are not enough. I need the rest of it, the soul of it, the geography of it – "*with love.*"

not really

He told me they would never know what hit them. Mice can't live in the house, after all. But when he spoke with amusement about the one little broken body that had been crushed by two traps, I knew two things. He had been wrong. And he hadn't really cared.

What is the "really" about? Everyone around me "cares" but not really. The gap between the two has opened up and swallowed me. Now I sit in my dark and solitary pit, with all sorts of kindly (and some not-so-kindly) faces peering over the edge from time to time, thinking (I presume) that I'm not doing very well and they're sure as heck not going to fall into the same trap I did.

They care about slaughtered horses and beaten pigs. Not really about skewered piglets. About mother turtles and endangered snakes. Not really about experimentally sickened rodents.

I understand the "not really" – it's the shield against insanity, and when we need it, we need it. But hold it up instead to protect ourselves from the onslaught of compassion, and we will find our hearts gradually turning to stone within our chests.

What was it that finally pierced my defences so that compassion could flow through? If I can figure that out, will I be able to chisel away at the defences of others? Do I want their hearts to break, when I haven't yet learned how to live with a broken-open heart?

But the animals are being broken by our hands. So yes, until that changes, let every human shield fail, and every human heart shatter.

without a thought

It was only a spider. Why do tears flow as I remember him? He was there in a quiet corner of my life, week by week discovered and allowed to remain, permitted to live, a comfort to me in my loneliness. Dependable, present.

And then one day in a moment of common sense, I pointed the vacuum and erased him from the neatness of my home.

Now his shadow mars instead a corner of my memory, lurks there with all those other innocent beings I have swept out of this world without a thought. The great silent pile of their tiny broken bodies making an unsightly mess in my conscience.

I am thinking now.

on the threshold

i have been pausing on this threshold a long time
i am tempted to look back – at all the good that is out there in the sunshine
at the panda face gazing up in love and devotion
golden puppyhood sprawled in the grass
blazing white glory shimmering on the dock
baby-trust enfolded in a child's arms
so many exquisite treasures captured on my little scraps of memories

But instead I know it is time to enter that place where I first encountered
the darkness, where the horror first gripped me by the throat.

still i pause just this little moment longer on the threshold
while i say good-bye to the sunshine

Awakening

the end for me

What I remember is the smile. Its body lay ravished, split open to reveal the source of each consumable body part, but the face looking towards the camera wore a smile. I kept that flyer from the supermarché for a long time, ready to pull it out and amuse our visitors – look at what people in this country find appealing to their appetites, can you imagine?! Ha, ha.

Birds in the marché hung fully intact so that purchasers would not be cheated. Limp testimony from heads and feet which only hours earlier had served their own purposes.

Whole grocery aisles devoted to *cheval* – ah, my childhood friends.

Despite a lifetime of practice, I found myself unable to keep my blinders in place any longer. They were slipping from my eyes, and I began to see that what was on my plate was staring back at me.

Meanwhile, that smile hung disembodied in my consciousness. I could not banish it.

And then one day we found ourselves stopped behind a truck, its back doors wide open. That which had been severed from the smile hung there instead.

Row after row of naked bodies, exposed, raw, unspeakably wronged. That was the end for me.

It's as though I keep seeing the same suffering eyes looking back at me through different bodies.

Twyla Francois

what has the power?

If I painted a building, would I dare to paint the horror? One great big mural with all the suffering on it. Like the walls in the Portuguese restaurant, covered with larger-than-life images tracing the whole unspeakable story, from happy families of sows with their playful babies, to tiny skewered bodies bleeding for your culinary pleasure. The people all around me feasted on those baby pigs, and though they glanced up from time to time, they remained strangely blind to the haunting eyes staring down at them. I, newly awakened, ate my bread and salad, and grieved for those broken bodies and their desolate mothers.

From that moment to this, I have longed to understand what changed me and what could change others. What has the power to stop the horror.

So if I painted a building, what could I paint that would make a difference? Great cruel strokes of black and red for all to see? Grasp the whole world and pull it down into the same grief I am drowning in? Is this what I have become, a messenger of ugliness and sadness, a thief of comfort, a prophet no one wants to hear?

When faced with horror, how can anyone paint pastels anymore? In the midst of a holocaust, how can art exist at all, other than for rescue's sake?

Rescue. How can I translate screams into images large enough for people to see?

Perhaps what I need to paint are eyes. Suffering eyes. And the change will come when one person looks into one creature's eyes and *sees* the suffering there.

To a man whose mind is free there is something even more intolerable in the sufferings of animals than in the sufferings of men. For with the latter it is at least admitted that suffering is evil and that the man who causes it is a criminal. But thousands of animals are uselessly butchered every day without a shadow of remorse. If any man were to refer to it, he would be thought ridiculous.

Romain Rolland

who will speak?

I have no idea where it happened, when it happened, why it happened. Only that there was a pig and there was a man. And there was torture. I forced myself to keep watching, not to turn away, not to close my eyes, not to protect myself. If that pig had no choice but to suffer that bewildered senseless prolonged agony in her death, what right had I to look away?

There are countless more undercover videos, a pornography of cruelty, each event unspeakable, unimaginable. I remain to this day desperate with the need to close my eyes against the sliding-scale cruelty of the whole damn stinking mess of it. The mere description of what is in those videos throws me to the floor in agony and rage.

What has become of me? More importantly, given what is happening to *them*, why does it matter one bit what becomes of *me*?

It matters, because if I can no longer go on, then who will speak for them? Who will *rage* for them? Who will grieve for them?

I *will not* abandon the suffering eyes.

An infant crying in the night
An infant crying for the light
And with no language but a cry.

Alfred Tennyson

We feed on babies, though not on our own.

Robert Louis Stevenson

I wish to God

Trucks frighten me now. They are my accusers. Eyes look out from them, straight into mine as I travel behind. Babies cry in the heat and thirst and fear of them. I heard them – I thought they were human babies – but they were pigs piled layer upon layer, no voice but a cry, exactly a baby's cry. The sun was blazing down, no air, no water, the truck parked at the rest stop. I saw and I heard and I wished to God I had not. I drove away helpless into my own world, my soul shrivelling within me, those baby screams ripping my heart open.

There was another time and another place where others stood by and watched and did nothing, just like me. History has accused them. I don't have to wait for history. I accuse myself.

As we talked of freedom and justice one day for all,
we sat down to steaks. I am eating misery, I thought,
as I took the first bite. And spit it out.

Alice Walker

my story

It is like there is a crack in the world, and I am in danger of falling through. Over the past few years, the crack has opened wider and wider, and new fissures have spread out from it, until in every direction there it stretches to my visible horizon. The crack is the pain of everything around me. I, who feel the pain of others, don't know what to do, don't know how to stop it happening, don't know how to avoid falling in at every turn.

Why must we hurt anything – everything? – merely to satisfy our appetite? Is our craving that imperative? Our senses so dull that all we feel is what goes on in our own small truth? What if we let in the truth of others? Of you, the "other" whose life is in our hands. I make my eyes lock with your eyes, and the vulnerability there is like a knife to my soul. How can we steal from you? Rip away from you everything that matters to you? Who told us we could do that?

I used to be able to do that. Not directly but through an agent, someone who did the killing for me. And then one day the intermediary fiction dropped away as I sat in a car behind a truck, the back doors open and your bodies – things stripped of you – hanging there in all the horrible truth that was yours to endure at my hands. My hands, though I had ceded the guilt to others for so long. Now it was my guilt and I looked it straight in its blood and bones and sinews.

And so the crack in your world became the crack in mine, and I walk down grocery aisles with tears coursing through my veins. I desperately shield my mind from monstrous stories that begin with playful babies who don't know how little time they have before their torture begins. The thirst, the heat, the cold, the starvation, the fear. And you, helpless against violence, still a screaming baby, billions of screaming babies. Someone's baby, ripped from her side to be stripped of life to feed the stomachs of others who don't even care what was stolen from you.

How does this story ever end? How do I go on with the blood of innocents pulsing through my consciousness in every meal I share with meat-eaters across from me? With your screams hollowing out my conscience every time I avert my eyes rather than speak of my grief for you.

Billions and billions. And me, with nothing for your agony but my tears.

Can you drink from the cup that I am going to drink from?

Jesus

the cup

Jesus left the city and went, as he usually did, to the Mount of Olives; and the disciples went with him. When he arrived at the place, he said to them, "Pray that you will not fall into temptation."

Then he went off from them about the distance of a stone's throw and knelt down and prayed. "Father," he said, "if you will, take this cup of suffering away from me. Not my will, however, but your will be done." An angel from heaven appeared to him and strengthened him. In great anguish he prayed even more fervently; his sweat was like drops of blood falling to the ground.

Rising from his prayer, he went back to the disciples and found them asleep, worn out by their grief. He said to them, "Why are you sleeping? Get up and pray that you will not fall into temptation."

Repeated twice, in the face of grief. What is the temptation?

Witness

beginning somewhere

Put it off, cram it down, cover it up, turn aside, close my eyes, rot away from the inside out. Do anything but see. Do anything but think. Do anything but know.

But I do know.

A chicken is decapitated by an automated feeding cart, and I am wrenched out of the disintegrating shelter of my own world and flung irretrievably into the helplessness of hers.

I have seen and heard things that ought not to be. Love for the suffering ones has burst my heart open, and my grief has spilled out everywhere. I now have no way back to my personal garden of innocence and comfort without bringing them with me. Their suffering has become my suffering, their peace my peace. I know no other way to love.

Suffering eyes speak to me. I will no longer abandon them. Whatever it costs me, I will find words for their agony, words strong enough to move the oppressors to mercy, words powerful enough to rescue those I love.

We sin against life when we treat animals as though they were only things. Is the heart, beating under a covering of bristles, feathers, or wings, any the less a heart?

Jean Paul Richter

the lucky ones

The word "evil" has gone out of favour, as it has done before in human history. But something by that name keeps rearing up and looking me in the eye with its cold stare of nothingness. I don't know what other word to use as I begin to break through the barriers I once constructed for my self-preservation, and choose instead to see.

Evil thrust its cold fist into my chest as I watched a documentary about the poultry industry. This was the first time I truly understood what I had heard decades earlier about the journalist Malcolm Muggeridge. He had become a vegetarian, not because he believed it was morally wrong to eat animals, but because of the mere existence of factory farms. As long as there was such a thing in the world, he would not participate in the consumption of animals. A simple protest, so easy to do, so powerful if everyone did the same. Then someday, if ever the atrocity of assembly-line massacre is finally eradicated from this world, *then and only then* might it be appropriate to consider whether humans are justified in consuming less brutally obtained flesh.

And so I allow my mind to return to that moment when I sat in my comfortable living room and witnessed the horror for the very first time. Cold fists repeatedly reaching down and grabbing. Conveyer belt filled with living beings. Soft pretty bits of fluff. Babies just getting to know the world. That evil world where cold eyes look and pick and sort, and all the little boy bodies drop into grinders. Peeping with bewilderment, and then just bits of blood and bone, and soft feathers floating.

And the most horrible part of this whole horrible business has just dawned on me – those were the lucky ones.

We have enslaved the rest of the animal creation,
and have treated our distant cousins in fur and feathers so badly
that beyond doubt, if they were able to formulate a religion,
they would depict the Devil in human form.

William Ralph Inge

who are we?

Night after night the images have haunted me, day after day I have felt screams rising in my throat with the sickness of what I forced myself to see. And now I must think about those images again, let them rise to the surface, find words for the unspeakable, give testimony against my own kind. Damning evidence for the truth of William Ralph Inge's damning words.

The tiny baby piglet screaming with pain as his testicles are ripped from his body.

An endless line of chickens, alive and conscious, bodies suspended upside down, long dangling necks and terrified heads hanging helpless. The no-mercy of automated horror advancing them relentlessly towards the circling saw, like the villainous climax of some old-style silent movie. Except that here the terror and pain are real, and there is no rescue, and the cold hard steel slices its way through one last-breathing throat after another after another after another after another after another. And the horror of it makes my grief itself feel like a sacrilege, for it is my kind who are doing this.

And then there was that one free-range chicken, "humanely" slaughtered. Placed upside down in a cone. Helpless. Desperate panicked terrified defenceless. Her frantic struggling legs are what I will forever remember when I think of this whole litany of torments.

Aware of exactly what we are doing, yet we do it anyway. Capable of imagining ourselves into the pain and terror of our victims, yet we don't.

This is who we are.

the snake

The car ahead of me drove over a snake. I saw what became of it, its front portion writhing in agony, its back portion crushed to the pavement. And I, crazed with the horror of it, lacked the courage to go back and carry out the unthinkable kindness. That one poor suffering creature just like all those others, broken in pain and terror, death their only deliverance. And that final indignity, pathetic body that once was a life, exposed in disfigured nakedness before uncaring eyes.

I have heard allegations – and confessions – of this deliberately done. I wonder at how this mirrors the larger scene, that big picture of humanity crushing and mangling, inflicting pain and stealing the light of life. All for pleasure's sake, for some twisted sense of power or some refined sensation of taste. The cries of our victims rise up against us, and our answer is a mockery.

Would all other beings on this planet be better off without us? Surely we can find another way, a way to become allies and family, a way for the whole world to be better off because we are in it.

Bullies or guardians? Our strength has determined that we must be one or the other.

feeble

I'm stuck. In the mud. Of my muddied mind.

It's those baby elephants. I can't go there. Rage is waiting for me if I go there. Helpless, impotent rage. A world of evil, and I sit here with nothing I can do about it. Except spew out pointless drivel on a page. For what?

My fingers keep punching out the letters, punching out the words, feeble jabs in the air, while humans like me are ripping apart great beautiful beings and leaving the babies to die of grief.

Human. Mean, ugly thing to be.

What good are words when babies are longing for their mothers?

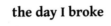

the day I broke

"South Korea Buries One Million Pigs Alive"

Whatever you did to them, you did to me.

Jesus

your torment

Where has hope for the future gone? Down in the pit with the pigs? Down on the floor with my screams, trying to block out theirs? What good are these words I write? Try offering words to that pig falling into the pit. Along with the million others. Let words be buried along with them as the dirt piles over their broken limbs, smothering out that last glimpse of the sun, choking off their short miserable lives – see how much good words will do for them.

Here, pigs, breathe these words, let these words comfort you in your terror and agony. Words, stupid human words – here, let them ease your torment.

Lord, why are you silent? Why are you always silent?

Shusaku Endo

despair

It is as if I went to fetch water, good clean water to drink and to share, and instead I fell in and plunged heart-first beneath waves of dirt and blood and shame and guilt. No way out.

Waters have covered the whole earth, the flood is not receding, there are no mountaintops left anywhere, and I have no ark. Like those tragic figures in an ancient painting, I find myself reaching out – too late, too late – as the ark goes by.

The waters cover us – all the tortured creatures sinking beside me – all of us abandoned together. Closing our eyes to the betrayal of that distant rainbow.

I can't breathe, and God is silent.

Dear Father, hear and bless,
Thy beasts and singing birds.
And guard with tenderness,
Small things that have no words.

Traditional prayer

sanctuary

Hope took me by surprise today, appeared before me in unanticipated simplicity.

A young couple returned to the place where earlier they had discovered a nest of orphaned baby rabbits. Gently carrying the limp little bodies in a shoebox, they walked past me mournfully in solemn recognition that it had been too late for one of the lovely silken-grey creatures. I watched as this young man and woman let their hearts be wounded and their afternoon be spent in rushing these babies to sanctuary many kilometres away.

As I watched them, I realized that whatever was to become of our tender hope for these fragile little rabbit lives, Hope had found its way back to me in the form of two human beings with loving hearts and a rescue mission.

They have no way of knowing that they were also rescuing me.

O gather up the brokenness
And bring it to me now
The fragrance of those promises
You never dared to vow

Behold the gates of mercy
In arbitrary space
And none of us deserving
The cruelty or the grace

O solitude of longing
Where love has been confined
Come healing of the body
Come healing of the mind

O see the darkness yielding
That tore the light apart
Come healing of the reason
Come healing of the heart

O longing of the branches
To lift the little bud
O longing of the arteries
To purify the blood

And let the heavens hear it
The penitential hymn
Come healing of the spirit
Come healing of the limb

Leonard Cohen

I remember you

I drive behind you, gazing into your questioning eyes. You ask me "why?" and all I can answer is "I'm sorry." I let them take you away to kill you, and always I remember your eyes asking me why.

The elephant is struck by a train, the horse pushed to its death, the puppy tossed off a cliff, dogs' legs dislocated and moon bears tortured, turkeys and pigs and cows and calves beaten raped pierced torn crushed broken and there is no accounting and no one to grieve and no meaning to be found. And so my words become gibberish, frantic with grief and rage.

Gathering sorrows like sheaves, piling them up in heaps all around myself, one great big fortress of suffering enveloping me, wondering how to escape without abandoning those who have no choice.

We were told that fish had no feelings, and we killed them with abandon. Sometimes I would give a fleeting thought to whether these animals suffered as they lay gasping on the shore.

Steve Hindi

gasping

I happened upon a cloud of newly hatched fish at the end of our dock. Slowly lowering my arm into the middle of the gentle miracle, I watched with wonder as the cloud parted, then came together again, and one by one little nibbles of curiosity and hunger tasted my flesh and moved on. Now when I think of them, my heart constricts with anguish. A million pigs in one horrific event, millions of fish every single day. Slow agonized death in piles upon piles of flailing bodies, gasping mouths unable to process the oxygen surrounding them like a grave.

Sharks sink to the bottom of the ocean, their fins severed from their bodies to make soup. Still-living torsos buried alive in their own native waters.

And that one fish, still alive, though barely. Last desperate flailing on a diner's plate, captured on film along with the obscenity of human laughter in the face of a creature being buried alive.

It is in my opinion giving up the light of reason to assert that beasts are no more than mere machines. I think one must never have made any observation upon animals, not to distinguish in them the different cries of want, suffering, joy, fear, love, anger, and indeed all other affections of the mind or body; surely, it would be very strange, that they should so well express what they have no sense of!

Voltaire

heart of darkness

I keep wondering, as I write these reflections, whether I have finally reached the deepest place. Is *this* the worst there is, is *this* where the heart of darkness resides? Does *this* somehow explain the endless torrent of senseless cruelties? But perhaps it is not in numbers, not in ferocity, not in scale, that I will find an answer. Perhaps it is in coldness. In nothingness. In the *thing-ness* that turns hearts to stone and spews out the unthinkable.

Contrary to what it may look like, I *do* try to protect my heart. I have to, it's been so badly shattered. Into a million pieces with the pigs, into bleeding fragments on the floors of countless slaughterhouses. I can't escape the knowledge, and now my heart is so broken that I don't know how it continues to rhythm out life for me at all. But even as I try desperately to numb my heart with trivial distractions, to bandage it up with soothing trifles, to continue sending it out in gentle pulses to loved ones who still need me, out leaps the next unlooked-for horror.

One day it came with laughter, in the middle of a feel-good Christmas news story. "Turkey-bowling," they called it. My words freeze in my mouth. Not one word I can think of seems adequate to this desecration, this reduction of bodies that used to be beautiful to objects in some obscene human game.

Wild turkeys stroll around our home, babies following mothers in meandering rivers of contentment. I hope for them, that they will be safe. I tremble at their vulnerability. They live and they love, and they move freely in and out of my world as they choose.

They are not things. They are not things. *They are not THINGS.*

If you cannot attain to knowledge without torturing a dog,
you must do without knowledge.

George Bernard Shaw

Can it be right to water the tree of knowledge with blood?
Does concern for human welfare justify the ruthless torture of our
poorer relations, whose little treasure we would tear from them
in order to add to our own wealth? Who would dare live a life
wrung from the agonies of tortured innocents?

George MacDonald

the beast below

"The Beast Below" episode of *Doctor Who* contained a dark, ugly secret. A spaceship had been constructed on the back of a captive star whale, an immense beast forced by means of continual torture to carry a human colony through space. The colonists did what they thought necessary, and escaped the pain of their remorse by muting the creature's screams, and by choosing artificially induced forgetfulness for themselves. Exactly as we do in our world.

All of our institutions, seemingly our very survival, everything dependent on the relentless infliction of continual suffering. As the guardians of that colony urged, the only way to bear the horror of what we are doing is to push the "forget" button. And as Doctor Who understood, the only way to change anything is to risk everything.

I still think of the rats whose last hours of life I heard described so matter-of-factly. The audience listened to the scientist with detached interest, while I felt my mundane existence suddenly plunged into a horror story. I looked around – was I the only one? Rats implanted with electrodes. Sleep waves detected, platform retracted, rats plunged into water. Platform restored, sleep waves detected again, platform retracted again. Over and over and over and over for days until they died. Then the autopsy to plunder their tiny bodies, to rip out scientific knowledge from their swollen, bleeding organs, to determine exactly how stress kills.

Was I the only one hearing an account of torture? Did no one else shed any tears over what these tidbits of knowledge had cost those helpless victims? Or did the taking of notes and the accumulation of facts somehow conceal the truth?

How many other experiments? How many for nothing, absolutely *nothing*? Most for feeble fragments of knowledge. A handful for life-saving discoveries. All built over a foundation of torment, serving the wants and requirements of humanity while the never-ending screams and whimpers of our weaker cousins are hidden away, muted, forgotten.

A dog sent into space to die a slow, terrified, solitary death. Primates used to test crash helmets. Rabbits immobilized, their eyes gradually and painfully burned away. Rats and mice deliberately sickened, drugged and discarded. And all of us benefitting, all of us living off the profits, and all of us – even those of us who cry at the horror of it all – deliberately pushing the "forget" button.

What would happen if we risked everything instead?

The worship of Knowledge has reached the point where its servants, people who are just as kind to their children as other people are, are prepared to put aside every scruple and subject innocent, helpless, pleading, speechless souls to such tortures whose mere description would make me guilty of cruelty to my listeners.

George MacDonald

for nothing

I listened to the radio for a few moments, then rushed to find pen and paper. I wrote down – word for word – the scientist's concluding observation about an experiment with sea urchins:

"Whenever we starved them, there was a high rate of cannibalism."

Does anyone else hear what I hear?

the camel

It took me a moment to grasp what the picture was showing. A photograph, spread over both pages, stark colours, a crowd of nameless faces blurring into the background as the one non-human being came into focus, and stopped my breath.

I gasp for words even now as my memory returns to that upstretched neck, open screaming mouth, terror-agonized eyes. My chest constricts with a desperate craving to obliterate the reality from my thoughts – but more, far more truly, from the world.

Or if not that, then I long to close my eyes and sink into the same darkness that moments later enfolded that broken innocent body.

I wish I could rewind everything, prevent that one poor friendless creature from ever knowing such terror and pain in those last ravaged moments of its life. But I can't make the fact of it go away. Nor the facts of all our unspeakable atrocities and calculated cruelties.

So I numb my mind day and night, watch the hours go by, the days, and try to live right and kind. But my breath comes broken now.

How can I hold on to hope if caring people around me are able to look into the eyes of that camel, quietly close the book, and walk away? The camel has broken my back, and I have no strength left.

the end of words

I saw your photograph in a magazine. Powerful black bull rhinoceros transfigured into a helpless, unrecognizable mass of suffering. Raw wounds where your horns used to be. Your shoulder shattered, your glory mutilated, your eye fading with sadness, you bear in your dying visage the agonies of all those helpless creatures whose torture and slaughter I have witnessed.

Always as I write these words for the sake of rescue, I know there is nothing my words can do to change what happened to any of you. And that makes my words a blasphemy, because they are not for you.

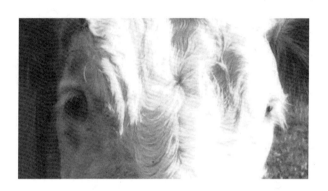

Other Voices

All beings tremble before violence.
All fear death. All love life.
See yourself in others.
Then whom can you hurt?
What harm can you do?

Buddha

On the Eating of Flesh
Plutarch

Can you really ask what reason Pythagoras had for abstaining from flesh? For my part I rather wonder both by what accident and in what state of soul or mind the first man who did so, touched his mouth to gore and brought his lips to the flesh of a dead creature, he who set forth tables of dead, stale bodies and ventured to call food and nourishment the parts that had a little before bellowed and cried, moved and lived. How could his eyes endure the slaughter when throats were slit and hides flayed and limbs torn from limb? How could his nose endure the stench? How was it that the pollution did not turn away his taste, which made contact with the sores of others and sucked juices and serums from mortal wounds? It is the man who first began these practices that one should seek out, not him who all too late desisted.

Or would everyone declare that the reason for those who first instituted flesh-eating was the necessity of their poverty? What wonder if, contrary to nature, we made use of the flesh of beasts when even mud was eaten and the bark of trees devoured, and to light on sprouting grass or the root of a rush was a piece of luck? But you who live now, what madness, what frenzy drives you to the pollution of shedding blood, you who have such a superfluity of necessities? Why slander the earth by implying that she cannot support you? Are you not ashamed to mingle domestic crops with blood and gore? You call serpents and panthers and lions savage, but you yourselves, by your own foul slaughters, leave them no room to outdo you in cruelty; for their slaughter is their living, yours is a mere appetizer.

It is certainly not lions and wolves that we eat out of self-defence; on the contrary, we ignore these and slaughter harmless, tame creatures without stings or teeth to harm us, creatures that, I swear, Nature appears to have produced for the sake of their beauty and grace.

But nothing abashed us, not the flower-like tinting of the flesh, not the persuasiveness of the harmonious voice, not the cleanliness of their habits or the unusual intelligence that may be found in the poor wretches. No, for the sake of a little flesh we deprive them of sun, of light, of the duration of life to which they are entitled by birth and being.

We declare, then, that it is absurd for them to say that the practice of flesh-eating is based on Nature. If you declare that you are naturally designed for such a diet, then first kill for yourself what you want to eat. Do it, however, only through your own resources, unaided by cleaver or cudgel of any kind or axe. Rather, just as wolves and bears and lions themselves slay what they eat, so you are to fell an ox with your fangs or a boar with your jaws, or tear a lamb or hare in bits. Fall upon it and eat it still living, as animals do.

But apart from these considerations, do you not find here a wonderful means of training in social responsibility? Who could wrong a human being when he found himself so gently and humanely disposed toward other non-human creatures?

A Dog's Tale
Mark Twain

One day I was standing a watch in the nursery. That is to say, I was asleep on the bed. The baby was asleep in the crib, which was alongside the bed, on the side next the fireplace. It was the kind of crib that has a lofty tent over it made of a gauzy stuff that you can see through. The nurse was out, and we two sleepers were alone. A spark from the wood-fire was shot out, and it lit on the slope of the tent. I suppose a quiet interval followed, then a scream from the baby woke me, and there was that tent flaming up toward the ceiling! Before I could think, I sprang to the floor in my fright, and in a second was half-way to the door; but in the next half-second I was back on the bed again. I reached my head through the flames and dragged the baby out by the waist-band, and tugged it along, and we fell to the floor together in a cloud of smoke; I snatched a new hold, and dragged the screaming little creature along and out at the door and around the bend of the hall, and was still tugging away, all excited and happy and proud, when the master's voice shouted:

"Begone you cursed beast!" and I jumped to save myself; but he was furiously quick, and chased me up, striking furiously at me with his cane, I dodging this way and that, in terror, and at last a strong blow fell upon my left foreleg, which made me shriek and fall, for the moment, helpless; the cane went up for another blow, but never descended, for the nurse's voice rang wildly out, "The nursery's on fire!" and the master rushed away in that direction, and my other bones were saved.

By and by came my little puppy, and then my cup was full, my happiness was perfect. It was the dearest little waddling thing, and so smooth and soft and velvety, and had such cunning little awkward paws, and such affectionate eyes, and such a sweet and innocent face.

The master's friends came, a whole twenty of the most distinguished people. They discussed optics, as they called it, and whether a certain injury to the brain would produce blindness or not, but they could not agree about it, and said they must test it by experiment. They took the puppy to the laboratory, and I limped three-leggedly along, too, feeling proud, for any attention shown the puppy was a pleasure to me, of course. They discussed and experimented, and then suddenly the puppy shrieked, and they set him on the floor, and he went staggering around, with his head all bloody, and the master clapped his hands and shouted:

"There, I've won – confess it! He's as blind as a bat!"

And they all said:

"It's so – you've proved your theory, and suffering humanity owes you a great debt from henceforth," and they crowded around him, and wrung his hand cordially and thankfully, and praised him.

But I hardly saw or heard these things, for I ran at once to my little darling, and snuggled close to it where it lay, and licked the blood, and it put its head against mine, whimpering softly, and I knew in my heart it was a comfort to it in its pain and trouble to feel its mother's touch, though it could not see me. Then it dropped down, presently, and its little velvet nose rested upon the floor, and it was still, and did not move any more.

The animals of the world exist for their own reasons.
They were not made for humans.

Alice Walker

wherever a heart beats
James Oliver Curwood

I have twenty-seven guns – and I have used them all. I stand condemned as having done more than my share toward extermination. But that does not lessen the fact that I have learned; and in learning I have come to believe that if boys and girls and men and women could be brought into the homes and lives of wild birds and animals as their homes are made and their lives are lived we would all understand at last that wherever a heart beats it is very much like our own in the final analysis of things. To see a bird singing on a twig means but little; but to live a season with that bird, to be with it in courting days, in matehood and motherhood, to understand its griefs as well as its gladness means a great deal. And in my books it is my desire to tell of the lives of the wild things which I know as they are actually lived. It is not my desire to humanize them. If we are to love wild animals so much that we do not want to kill them *we must know them as they actually live.* And in their lives, in the *facts* of their lives, there is so much of real and honest romance and tragedy, so much that makes them akin to ourselves that the animal biographer need not step aside from the paths of actuality to hold one's interest.

The intelligence's enlightenment by love
is a terrible teaching (in the literal sense of the word).
Contemplate what happens to those who have been
deeply illuminated by love!

George Grant

Bruno: A New Perspective on Happy Cows
Alisa Rutherford-Fortunati

Sitting in my office in downtown Boston, I stared out the frosted glass and dreamed of Italy. A small farm filled with animals wandering in green pastures, clucking at my heels, waiting eagerly to have grain and hay thrown into their troughs. One more month, and I would be volunteering on a small organic dairy farm nestled in the pristine Italian countryside.

While I had been a vegetarian for five years at that point, I loved cheese, and the idea of being as close to the source as possible was enticing. I wanted to know where my food came from, to be part of its growth and life. What could be more idyllic than to live my life by the chimes of the church bell and oscillating calls of impatient cows?

When I first arrived, the farm was everything I had hoped for. Each morning I awoke to the church bells I had dreamed of. After a classic European breakfast, complete with fresh milk, I trudged up the hill to clean out the cow and goat stalls, and feed the chickens. Then, if the weather suited, I would go for a walk in the woods with the goats, or down to the pasture with the cows. It was serene.

The story I truly want to tell you though is about one cow in particular, a cow to whom I owe a great deal:

Bruno.

The first time I met this funny cow, I had to jump out of the way as he attempted to lick my jacket. Once, when I was distracted, his tongue caught me on the arm. I would later compare the sensation to being licked by a wet Brillo Pad.

Bruno never walked down to the grazing pasture with us because he was a bull and too unpredictable, but each morning he waited impatiently for his share of milk, alongside a female cow who was pregnant with her first calf and Max, a smaller variety of bull.

I loved giving them their morning milk. Never once did I question the inherent strangeness in taking the milk from Max's mother, and the other two lactating cows, walking 100 feet and then feeding a portion of this milk out of a bottle to Max and out of a trough to Bruno. They were simply adorable animals that I was thrilled to feed.

These cows were "lucky" that they even got milk, although at times it was partially powdered or had an egg in it when there was not enough milk for both us and them.

Life went on like this for a month and a half. And then a piece of paper entitled "Bruno" started floating around the house.

- Paul 50 Kg
- Nichole 125 Kg
- Lupo 25 Kg

They were dividing up Bruno's body for consumption. My host, who was a vegetarian, said it was her least favorite part of owning a dairy farm. She had warned me, before I even arrived, that she had to sell some animals to pay for the care of the others, but I never fully understood what that meant. At the time I spoke of praying for their souls and being glad they had lived a good life, a happy life.

After another two weeks, the list was complete. My host said that the following Saturday, a friend would be coming to help her move Bruno to a temporary holding stall before he was put in the butcher's truck.

As Saturday morning approached, my fellow volunteers and I waited eagerly to see if Bruno would put up a fight. He still had his horns and had quickly grown to a hefty size under our care.

My host and her friend took off up the hill, their breath hanging in the air above the slowly rumbling tractor. Those of us left in the house waited for the sound of the tractor to disappear and then paced, paused and pondered its return. The time seemed to drag on forever. Finally we heard the tractor slowly descending. As it rounded the bend, we saw that there was no fighting bull, no struggle. Bruno, tied to the tractor, slowly walked behind, calmly being led by someone he trusted. We were the only mothers he had ever really had the chance to know. Why would he put up a fight? Why would he distrust the hands that fed him and scratched his chin?

The next morning he was gone.

A day later, his body came home in pieces. Being a vegetarian at the time, my host did not ask if I wanted to try the meat I had helped to "raise," but my fellow volunteers were asked if they wanted to have hamburgers that night. They hesitated, which was one of the few things at the time that made the acid in my stomach turn. If they could eat meat in general, why couldn't they eat an animal they had helped to raise? They finally relented and dined on Bruno that night.

As I left the house that evening, the smell of hamburger still clinging to my clothes, I almost tripped over a long white object lying in the driveway. It was Bruno's spine, left as a treat for the dogs. Tiny bits of pink flesh were still clinging in between the vertebrae. I could not connect this piece of flesh and bone to the animal I had loved. Instead, I simply turned away, went into my room, and fell asleep.

I awoke the next morning and wrote to family and friends how his death had not bothered me – a lie, although I did not know it at the time. I wrote that "I will be a veggie until the day I die, but living and working on this farm has allowed me to accept death as a natural part of life."

It took me months to realize that I shut down that night, that to simply turn away from the bones of this animal – an animal I had loved and cared for – meant turning off a part of myself. Upon rereading my emails and blogs from this time, anger and shame well in my heart, and tears are not far behind. I realize now that I was complacent towards the existence of these creatures. I accepted the use and abuse of their bodies for my desire for milk and others' desire for meat. And now, I find that the only way I can ask for forgiveness for my part in Bruno's death is by telling his story.

This is not the story of a factory farm; it is the story of a beautiful farm with "free range" animals who seemed to be "happy." They were labeled "happy" because someone cared enough about them to "minimize" the abuse of their bodies before they were killed.

Now, as I go about my life, awake and vegan, pictures of these animals float across my mind: Bruno, Ortensia (the first cow I ever saw skip with joy), Mariolana (my favorite goat struggling to carry her last kid) and Max (the smallest calf and the next to be sold for meat). I see their shining eyes eagerly waiting for me to deliver their morning milk, hoping for a bit of green hay or a scratch on the chin. I know these were animals capable of being happy and that they had this chance stolen from them.

An animal's eyes have the power to speak a great language.

Martin Buber

On a Mother's Love
Holly Cheever

When I first graduated from Cornell's School of Veterinary Medicine, I went into a busy dairy practice in Cortland County, New York. One of my clients called me with a puzzling mystery: his Brown Swiss cow, having delivered her fifth calf naturally on pasture the night before, brought the new baby to the barn and was put into the milking line, while her calf was once again removed from her. Her udder, though, was completely empty, and remained so for several days. As a new mother, she would normally be producing close to one hundred pounds (12.5 gallons) of milk daily; yet, despite the fact that she was glowing with health, her udder remained empty. She went out to pasture every morning after the first milking, returned for milking in the evening, and again was let out to pasture for the night, but never was her udder swollen with the large quantities of milk that are the hallmark of a recently calved cow.

I was called to check this mystery cow two times during the first week after her delivery and could find no solution to this puzzle. Finally, on the eleventh day post calving, the farmer called me with the solution. He had followed the cow out to her pasture after her morning milking, and discovered the cause: she had delivered twins, and in a bovine "Sophie's Choice," she had brought one to the farmer and kept one hidden in the woods at the edge of her pasture, so that every day and every night, she stayed with her baby – the first she had been able to nurture FINALLY – and her calf nursed her dry with gusto. Though I pleaded for the farmer to keep her and her bull calf together, she lost this baby too – off to the hell of the veal crate.

Think for a moment of the complex reasoning this mama exhibited: first, she had memory – memory of her four previous losses, in which bringing her new calf to the barn resulted in her never seeing him/her again. Second, she could formulate and then execute a plan: if bringing a calf to the farmer meant that she would inevitably lose him/her, then she would keep her calf hidden. Third – and I do not know what to make of this myself – instead of hiding both, which would have aroused the farmer's suspicion, she gave him one and kept one herself. I cannot tell you how she knew to do this. All I know is this: there is a lot more going on behind those beautiful eyes than we humans have ever given them credit for, and as a mother who was able to nurse all four of my babies and did not have to suffer the agonies of losing my beloved offspring, I feel her pain.

The Spirit of God has sent me to release the oppressed.

Jesus

22815
Nathan Runkle

For years, she stood in her crate alone, never knowing the warmth of the sun or the feel of grass under her hooves. Never a moment of play with others. Never a tender touch. Year after year, again and again, her piglets were taken from her. She could only watch helplessly as they screamed in pain while they were castrated and their tails cut off without painkillers. The cold metal bars that held her captive were unrelenting.

There was no comfort to be found in the dirty crate too small for her to even turn around or lie down comfortably. She would take a tiny step forward and another one back. She would gnaw on the bars that surrounded her.

Sow 22815 died, her body emaciated, covered with sores, and marked with spray paint for the trash.

Jane – one tiny chicken foot. . .
Twyla Francois

While in Toronto, Ontario, on investigation into a large-scale chicken slaughter plant located in the city, I saw an empty chicken transport trailer. It was completely clean (it had just gone through their pressure washer), except for one tiny chicken foot that had become lodged in one of the red and yellow crates. I thought it important to give the owner of this foot a name, and to tell her story as I imagine it might have been.

Jane was a baby broiler chicken who lived in a barren, crowded, filthy barn with 5,000 to 50,000 other baby birds. Bred to grow too quickly, she most likely suffered from crippling skeletal problems, and the foot that was left behind in the trailer could well have been part of a leg that was in constant pain.

When the day came for her to be trucked to slaughter, Jane would have still been a baby, blue-eyed and peeping, only 42 days old. Terrified, she would have been violently yanked by her feet and carried upside down with three or four other terrified birds and shoved roughly into a transport crate. Here in Canada, she could have been trucked for up to 36 hours without food or water in the cold and rain.

It was probably at the slaughterhouse that Jane's leg was amputated. Probably as she was being ripped from the crate, her foot jammed, and her body was pulled and separated from her leg. She would have screamed, but no one would have heard.

Inside the slaughterhouse, Jane's other leg was snapped into a shackle, where she hung, upside down from the conveyer belt, with her heart beating in terror, and her bleeding leg stump, and quite possibly she slipped from the shackle and fell to the floor before they cut her throat. With only one leg and one bleeding stump, she would have flopped around on the slippery surface of the kill floor, until someone kicked her, or threw her against the wall, or worse (as numerous investigations have shown).

If Jane was rehung in the shackle (as often happens), chances are she did not enter the electrified "stun" bath properly, but "properly" or otherwise, she suddenly feels to the core of her skeleton violent electric shocks pulsing and boring through her face, her eyes, her eardrums, her feathers, her skin, and her internal organs down through her legs and into her feet – into her foot and her leg stump. Now, she is not only mutilated but immobilized, because as research has shown, the electrified waterbath stunner is not designed to relieve pain and suffering, but only to paralyze a chicken's muscles so that her feathers will come out more easily after she (or he) is dead.

Conscious, mutilated, pulsing with the burning sensations of the electric shocks – unable to move or cry out – Jane was dumped with other chickens into a tank of scalding water, and no one saved her. All that remained was her story to tell, the story that I saw imprinted in her sad, helpless little foot left behind in the trailer, recalling the life of Jane, a baby broiler chicken who was tortured to death.

My Life as an Undercover Investigator
Cody Carlson

I was 25 years old when I began working as an undercover investigator. I picked up a state-of-the-art hidden camera and responded to an online want ad for a maintenance position at the biggest dairy farm in the Northeast. Maybe, I thought, it wouldn't be as bad as the undercover images I had seen of industrial egg, hog, and poultry farms. Maybe the worst factory farming cruelties hadn't fully taken over dairy farming yet. But by the end of my first day, I would realize how wrong I was.

Working at that·"farm," I learned that their 5,000 cows spent every day crowded in barren, manure-filled concrete barns. They were kept perpetually pregnant through artificial insemination, and routinely pumped full of antibiotics and hormones like rBST. Further, the cows were rife with swollen joint infections where their legs rubbed against the concrete, and suffered from heavy, inflamed udders. I watched every day as more cows collapsed at four or five years of age – a fraction of their natural lifespan – and were either left to die or shipped to slaughter. As for the many calves born as a by-product of dairy production, if they didn't freeze to death in an unattended tin shed, they were also shipped to slaughter within days of birth. These cows were being abused, neglected, and overdriven like disposable milk-producing machines.

That spring, I worked at a sow farm in central Pennsylvania for two months. After that, I spent a few weeks working at a pet store, learning how to eventually talk my way into about 50 puppy mills in Oklahoma, Texas, and Kansas. The next winter, I worked at a series of battery cage egg farms around Iowa. At each location, I found the same thing: countless animals suffering a fate worse than death.

The more I saw, the more I needed the world to recognize the weight of this injustice. I needed everyone to look into the eyes of a caged farm animal and recognize like I had that she feels the same pain, the same terror, and even the same potential joy as you or I. I watched young heifers and piglets wrestle and prance in their small concrete and steel pens, their instinctual and immutable enthusiasm for life momentarily triumphing over their cruel environment. Once, I watched as a mother sow cleverly engineered a prison break by loosening the hinges of her crate with her tongue until the front door fell off. After escorting out her piglets, the sow immediately began to do the same for another sow's door. My co-worker told me that several sows had orchestrated such "liberations" in the past, and that these sows had to be put down.

These bittersweet moments were few and far between. Mainly, I witnessed horrific scenes like mother pigs getting beaten with metal rods to force them back into farrowing crates after getting their first chance to walk in months. I watched them roar in helpless despair as their piglets were violently yanked from their teats and castrated in front of their faces. I watched countless egg-laying hens die of thirst, starvation, or trampling after their broken legs or wings became trapped in their cages. And I watched mother cows spend days bellowing for their stolen calves as if this was the first time it had happened. For me, these memories illustrate the tragedy of the modern animal farm. You need only look to see that these intelligent animals are paying an unfathomable cost to satisfy our habit for cheap meat, eggs and dairy.

Of course, individual workers aren't held responsible for these standard conditions. They are trained to ignore animal suffering, creating a work culture of apathy or even outright cruelty. Every facility had at least one person who tortured the animals for fun. These guys were troubled, and didn't make much effort to hide it from their co-workers. The scarier part was that nobody tried to stop them, or did anything more than tease them for their sadistic behavior. This was strange since many of the workers claimed that they cared about the animals, and admitted that they had to "get used to" working in the barns. Some told me privately about their frequent nightmares or their chronic health problems. They had to become desensitized just to make it through the day.

Once, a co-worker at a battery egg farm confronted me about my concern for the hens who were suffering from prolapsed uteri (a condition in which the birds' uteri are partially expelled from their bodies, and unable to be retracted). These herniated organs were getting tangled in the cages, causing an agonizingly slow death, and I had asked whether we were expected to provide veterinary care. In no uncertain terms, the worker accused me of being an undercover investigator. With my heart beating in my throat, I feigned annoyance, and told her to leave me alone and let me do my job. From then on, I only helped animals when no one was watching.

As a vegan and an animal lover, it was almost impossible to remain passive in the face of such cruelty, but that's exactly what my job required. As I worked, I reminded myself that this abuse was going to happen regardless of my presence, but would be documented if I stuck around by playing along.

Still, the experience was draining me. I was losing weight, sleeping fitfully, and forgetting how to interact with others socially.

After two years, I couldn't do it anymore.

A man can live and be healthy without killing animals for food; therefore, if he eats meat, he participates in taking animal life merely for the sake of his appetite. And to act so is immoral.

Leo Tolstoy

its little tail
Leo Tolstoy

I went into the compartment where small animals are slaughtered – a very large chamber with asphalt floor, and tables with backs, on which sheep and calves are killed. After me there entered a man, apparently an ex-soldier, bringing in a young yearling ram, black with a white mark on its neck, and its legs tied. This animal he placed upon one of the tables, as if upon a bed. The live ram was lying quietly, except that it was briskly wagging its short little tail and its sides were heaving more quickly than usual. The soldier pressed down its uplifted head gently, without effort; the butcher, still continuing the conversation, grasped with his left hand the head of the ram and cut its throat. The ram quivered, and the little tail stiffened and ceased to wave. The fellow, while waiting for the blood to flow, began to relight his cigarette, which had gone out. The blood flowed and the ram began to writhe. The conversation continued without the slightest interruption. It was horribly revolting. We cannot pretend that we do not know this. We cannot believe that if we refuse to look at what we do not wish to see, it will not exist. This is especially the case when what we do not wish to see is what we wish to eat.

Ashes

ashes

Like a kid in a candy shop.

I once saw a horse with that kind of happiness, throwing a ball around, tossing it, joying in it. Once I watched my dogs break free and career after a truck, wildly abandoning themselves to the rush of wind in their laughing faces. Without a worry, living just in this moment, happiness filling up cells and bones and blood, unadulterated, uncomplicated, free.

Like a baby elephant in his mother's embrace. Like a calf drinking from her mother. Like a lamb bounding in a field.

But these fleeting moments sink into the quicksand of my consciousness, and I am left with the chill that never lets me forget that all my living is a protest against the rotting of this world. There is no candy shop. No simple life for innocent beings.

Every taste of the world is bitter now, ashen. I hold it on my tongue, and I swallow, and I quell the rising nausea. I see a field of cows, perhaps contented, and I wonder if tomorrow they'll all be gone. I see a wagging tail, and I think of the moment when the wagging stopped for the trusting creature feeling its throat being cut. I cannot see happy photos of elephants, rhinos, whales and dolphins without thinking about what we do to them.

These are the ashes of my sorrow, marking and marring my soul as I try to make this world a sweeter place.

thanksgiving

I used to give thanks to the divine life-giver for the tortured, decapitated bird on the table. I used to salivate over the aroma, not smelling the suffering. I used to joke and laugh and see only an object at the centre of our celebration, not a stolen life.

Now I see piles of plastic-wrapped corpses in the supermarket, some still dripping their life-blood onto the counter in front of me. And lifeless broken body parts on the plates of those I love.

I find thoughts crowding my consciousness – who were you, how long did you live, did you have any happiness, was your whole life an agony, how did you die, were you afraid, did it hurt, I'm sorry.

I'm so bloody sorry.

the cemetery

A tiny gerbil lies buried in the woods next to our yard. She was loved, as children love, with simplicity and clarity. Her name is inscribed on a stone above her final resting place. Words were spoken by little ones, with truth and sadness. Bagpipes sounded nearby, a fitting coincidence.

But what of all those creatures whose bones are thrown into garbage bags, refuse from our tables, dishonoured, unloved? Or those lonely bodies lying on the road, their fates written in crushed limbs and broken postures. Who will grieve for *them*?

The ghosts of lives never treasured echo their misery in the pain of my heart. I wrestle to find any words left for me to speak, because so often now all I hear inside me is the silence after the screams. Silence excavating a death chamber within my deepest spirit. A catacomb to honour all those bones and ashes, a place where someone will care enough to remember them.

A little life dashes in front of my car and I have no time and it is gone. I see it unburied behind me, and I cry out for a long time.

Have I ever shed one single tear for all those others, for that immense pile of butchered bodies that my lifetime of consuming has heaped up in the accounting of my life? I can never have tears or vision or memory enough to weep for every pitiful creature whose cemetery was my stomach.

There was a tomb within a garden. The story tells of an angel who asked why Mary was crying. Look behind you - hope is more real than the grave. I try every day to believe that.

to be a life

She was probably seeking food for her little ones, oblivious to her own safety, focused solely on sustaining the lives of others. And I, because I had turned sooner rather than later, because I had waited just those number of seconds, no more no less, came across her path at that precise instant. And then she was gone.

I returned to face what I had done, and now that knowledge is a part of me, the vision of wings beating one last time, erratic, grasping the air as for a breath. Body suddenly heavy, never to be resurrected from the pavement, never again to know the freedom, the joy of defying the earth. All because we must travel in just this way, and can't help but trample.

I don't want the world to be this way. It is an awful thing to be a Life, said George MacDonald. It is. Weighted with solemn responsibility and desperate need. And yet "behind it all is tenderness and truthfulness and grace." How can we reach behind the hardness of life, and the hardness of our own hearts, to encounter that tenderness, truthfulness, grace?

I know of only one way. The Puritans said it best, with simplicity: "the broken heart is the healed heart."

playing god

I played Scrabble with my nine-year-old grandson yesterday, for the first time. He placed his word, then proudly turned to me and said, "I played god." I was taken aback by his inadvertent utterance of such a weighty expression. What a great opportunity to explain it to him, I thought. But I quickly realized that it has no child-friendly meaning.

Earlier that day I had woken up to a news item about pigs. Too groggy to defend myself against what was coming, too disoriented to remember the details, I nevertheless heard enough to go into my day heavy with grief. Genetically modified, unwanted, killed.

As I allow myself to think of those helpless creatures who did not choose to be born only to be killed, I remember the question asked of me earlier this week, "Well, if we don't eat farm animals, what should we do with them?"

What do we do with the billions of lives that we create only to destroy?

I find my mind returning to Mary Shelley's tragedy about Doctor Frankenstein's pathetic creature. The one who just wanted to be loved by his creator. The one whose creator would not take responsibility for him. The one who finally spoke these words:

"Hateful day when I received life!...Cursed creator!"

If the animals could speak, is that what they would say to us?

There will be no justice as long as man will stand with a knife or with a gun and destroy those who are weaker than he is.

Isaac Bashevis Singer

at the gate

Those who love you, Jesus, call you Lamb of God. They seek to honour you with a knife to the throat of your brothers and sisters, with your kindred's blood running from their mouths. They stand at your gate with the screams of their victims ringing in your ears. Your name is easy on their lips, but their garments are stained with blood.

How dare they stand at the gates of Love with a knife in their hands?

arches

Arches rise above the road to my home,
a multitude of trees on either side of my path
reaching out over my head to touch each other.
I walk along beneath this blessing,
and feel the warmth of this welcome home,
familiar and magical
like a cloak of protection and invisibility.
You are safe now. You are almost home.
Scurrying of small lives all about me –
rustle of leaves in the day
and alarms of flocks in the night –
all thanks to this canopy of life
hosting countless unseen living things.

Arches rise above pilgrims entering cathedrals,
reaching stone-cold and grey above each solitary searcher.
Capstones upholding our need for solidity, for comfort,
for protection from meaninglessness.
I walked beneath those arches
and shivered in the damp echoes all around me.
Everything unfamiliar and dark, like a tomb,
and yet I searched, longing for a home for my heart.
Slow murmurs and quiet pacing,
curious and desperate side by side in this vast cavern.
Voices of song rising,
shards of colour piercing down at our feet,
stone and wood all hard and cold and dead.

And then there are those other arches,
towering over cold coins and tormented bodies.
Children flock to them for plastic treasures and greasy fingers.
For decades I blinded myself and went there too
until gradually the scales fell from my eyes,
my heart was ripped open,
and I found my choking way out of that place of horror.
But everywhere I turn now, the twisted cruelty follows me.

There is no escape.
Not to cathedrals.
Not to the outstretch of trees above me.

And not to words such as these.
They emerge from my thoughts like little arrows,
reaching up into the sky, arching around,
and coming back down again to pierce my own heart.
These are the arches that I live with now.
Arcs of trajectory for thoughts that have nowhere to go
except back into my own already-wounded spirit.
Ascending perhaps a little less each time,
but descending ever deeper
with each effort I make to send them on their way.

Arches of my words above me –
I watch them rise and I prepare my heart
to receive them back into myself.
Am I doomed to this practice,
compelled to repeat it over and over again,
somehow hoping that this next time will be different?
The essence of madness, someone once called this kind of hope.

Again today I have shot my arrow up,
and I watch it now descend upon myself
to leave me just a little more bereft and alone
than I had been before offering these words
into the emptiness above me.

Weep with those who weep.

St. Paul

peripheral vision

Where can I go where everything is bright and sunshiny, with rainbows overhead? In children's dreams? No longer in mine. I am haunted by the cruelty and indifference that assault me at every turn. I close my eyes and hold my hands over my ears. But sudden horrors leap out at me from unexpected corners, and muffled sounds reduce screams of pain and terror to whimpers that leave me gasping with rage.

But there is something else in those dark and fearful corners, something that I glimpsed in the periphery of a dream. Divine eyes seeking mine. God's justice outraged and God's mercy grieved by the blood of innocents soaking the whole earth. Suffering Love at the heart of this broken universe.

I woke from my dream, and hope keeps slipping through my fingers, but with nowhere else to go, I continue to lean on Love.

Let me say it openly: we are surrounded by an enterprise of degradation,
cruelty, and killing which rivals anything that the Third Reich was
capable of, indeed dwarfs it, in that ours is an enterprise without end,
self-regenerating, bringing rabbits, rats, poultry, livestock ceaselessly
into the world for the purpose of killing them.

J. M. Coetzee

For the animals it is an eternal Treblinka.

Isaac Bashevis Singer

holocaust

I sat in the movie theatre
alone in the dark just a child
watching images
no child should see
piles of bodies
tortured flesh
naked and dumped
mountains of atrocity
accusing.

I sit now watching
again alone
gripping my own throat
with anguish
hooks and blades and
writhing bodies
agony and terror
rivers of screams
accusing.

as they see us

What if we saw ourselves as they see us? So many creatures willing to share earth with us, share air with us, share the joy of life with us. But we are not willing to share and so we tear them apart, and with them our own hearts, until all that is left are entrails of hopelessness, and our own bloodied future.

What have we become, and how can we ever make up for it?

And the disgrace of it is, that if ever they were released from their cages of torment, they would be very likely to forgive us.

But we would not deserve it.

shalom

We feel alone, estranged.
The torture of innocent creatures
is a torment to our souls,
while those around us look away
as if it doesn't matter.

Why is it *we* who are seen as ill?

We long to become whole again,
faith and awareness growing side by side within us,
strong and free,
our lives a unity of love
working for the *shalom* of this earth.

My throat, my soul is hoarse;
My heart is wither'd...

George Herbert

weary

Weary as a hot day,
shimmers of illusion
rising from blighted landscapes.
Helpless as suffering eyes
peering out from a truck,
patient misery moving
towards concealed violence.
Can I find relief,
some grand purpose,
or even some little one?
Just enough perhaps
to zip ink across pages
until some small arrow of truth
may at last dart out
and find even one tender heart
to pierce.

Parting Words

all I want

My Mom has been leaving me little by little. Fog surrounds her now, and growing darkness. She moves in her solitary awareness without guideposts, without something solid to hold on to. Pain comes to her through the mist, desperate and sad, without words to bring her the help she needs.

But one day, the sea of her bewilderment parted for a moment as a single urgent longing rose up from some place deep within her. Her one wish, her last clear message for me, her only daughter:

"All I want is for you to be happy."

My heart pains at the sound of it, at the essential Motherness of it, that one thing that every mother desperately wants for her every child. Some say that the last thing to go is hearing, that the deepest thing that stays with us is music. But since I heard those words, I think that for anyone who loves, *this* is the deepest and most enduring thing, whether words remain to bring that longing to light or not.

I just want you to be happy.

If we all said that, and if we meant it, as a mother would, for every one of this earth's little children, maybe I could taste a measure of what my mother wants for me.

Roots and Branches

The first part of *Suffering Eyes* is a collection of individual reflections arranged chronologically and thematically to tell the story of my awakening. In this second part of the book, I revisit my earlier reflections, providing the sources of quotations (and, as needed, fuller texts and original construction), while also thinking and feeling my way back into each one. In *Roots and Branches*, I share the roots of my writings, the experiences and underlying perspectives out of which they grew, and I explore many thoughts and impressions further, sketching in broad strokes those thematic outgrowths that branch naturally from the main body of the text.

It is my fervent hope that each of us will take the fine brush of our own thoughts and experiences to fill in the details of what an awakened life will look like in our individual situations.

dedication

My mother, Michelle Fauteux (Vann/Eaglesham/Woodburn/Clark), was the original vegetarian in our family. I wrote many of the reflections in this book during the last months of her life, as we lost her to Alzheimer's disease. Despite the increasing confusion of my mother's final years, she remained to the end firmly committed to a vegetarian diet, and passionate about embracing, protecting and caring for any vulnerable being that found its way into her life.

Mom had a special place in her heart for anyone who needed her. She always rooted for the underdog, and she raged against injustice done to anyone. She loved her rescued pets, and chose the sickliest ones because they needed her the most. She cared about the birds at her window, and the mice who found their way into her house. She cared about every helpless living creature, with all the passion in her heart.
- Excerpt from my eulogy for my mother.

opening quotes

Theodore Isaac Rubin, *One to One: Understanding Personal Relationships* (New York: The Viking Press, 1983).

George MacDonald, "Growth in Grace and Knowledge," in *George MacDonald in the Pulpit: The 'Spoken' Sermons of George MacDonald* (Whitethorn, CA: J. Joseph Flynn, 1996), 145.

Hasidic tale as told by Jacob Needleham in *Healing the Heart of Democracy: The Courage to Create a Politics Worthy of the Human Spirit*, by Parker J. Palmer (San Francisco: Jossey-Bass, 2011), 149-150.

Apologia

Suffering Eyes begins with a defence of empathy.

After decades of hiding from the truth, I finally chose to look at the suffering that humans inflict on animals. Immediately I became desperate to find a cure for the powerful emotions being awakened in me. I sought help from many sources but nothing was able to ease my agony. It was only when I gave up trying to escape that I learned to accept my capacity for empathy as a gift, and to exercise it as a responsibility. Connecting my wellbeing with that of the suffering ones, relinquishing the kind of personal consolation that would leave them behind, I began to walk forward into the pain. This book is the result.

Now it is a matter of great sadness to me that empathy needs defending at all. How else can healing come?

the bird / 15

We laughed at my mother. How could we?

We did not laugh in derision, but rather with affection. Nevertheless, the hardness of our hearts towards those my mother loved, denied us the right to laughter. This reflection is both an *apology* to my mother, and an *apologia* for empathy.

I continue to take delight in recounting (with tender laughter) those sweet and funny stories, but I do so now with a clearer conscience as I fully embrace the wisdom of my mother's unapologetic nurturing and passionate championship of every life in need of her.

> *There slowly grew up in me an unshakeable conviction that we have no right to inflict suffering and death on another living creature unless there is some unavoidable necessity for it, and that we ought all of us to feel what a horrible thing it is to cause suffering and death out of mere thoughtlessness. And this conviction has influenced me only more and more strongly with time. I have grown more and more certain that at the bottom of our heart we all think this, and that we fail to*

*acknowledge it and to carry our belief into practice chiefly
because we are afraid of being laughed at by other people as
sentimentalists, though partly also because we allow our best
feelings to get blunted. But I vowed that I would never be
afraid of the reproach of sentimentalism.*
- Albert Schweitzer, *Memoirs of Childhood and Youth*,
trans. C. T. Campion (New York: The MacMillan
Company, 1949), 31.

Looking Back

This section explores my experiences with animals over the first fifty
years of my life, from the vantage point of my present understanding.
My hope is that by tracing the roots of empathy in my own life, I may
nurture this capacity in the lives of others.

my mother's heart / 19

*I choose to be with. Let my own skin be wounded, let the blood of our separate
worlds be mingled.*

The soul of kindness is kindredness, the sense that everybody – every body
– shares a familial connection with me. As a student of Christian
theology, I have a special affinity with the "theology of the cross," an
understanding of God as intrinsically connected, sharing in the suffering
of creation, with. I believe that kinship with those who are suffering
requires no less of any of us.

Feeling my way through the painful reflections of this book, I often
experienced an overwhelming sense of isolation, even dislocation. I found
my despair reflected in the words of the fictional character Elizabeth
Costello, as she tries to explain her desperation over the suffering of
animals to her disapproving son in the novel *The Lives of Animals*:

> *I look into your eyes, into Norma's, into the children's, and I
> see only kindness, human-kindness. Calm down, I tell
> myself, you are making a mountain out of a molehill. This
> is life. Everyone else comes to terms with it, why can't you?
> Why can't you?*
> - J. M. Coetzee, *The Lives of Animals* (Princeton:
> Princeton University Press, 1999), 69.

What *is* the appropriate response to the suffering of others? Surely it is not to come to easy terms with it, to accept the pain as long as it does not touch our own bodies.

Theologians have identified the central dynamic of the Christian faith as the willing descent into the needs of others, with the intention of raising all of us together into a happier future. Douglas John Hall describes this "incarnational solidarity" with those who are suffering as the only way to "turn history towards life rather than death," and he defends this "sober recognition" of suffering as the necessary path towards healing:

> *The community that is moved by the gospel of the cross inevitably finds itself drawn towards earth's suffering ones.... It fastens upon that which negates and threatens the life of creation and upon God's intention, through incarnational solidarity with the world's suffering, to turn history towards life rather than death....If it concentrates upon suffering, it is not because this tradition manifests a morbid interest in pain, but because there is pain, because disintegrative pain is not part of what should be, and because there can be no healing that does not begin with the sober recognition of the reality of that which needs to be healed....The point of such a theology is not to wallow in despair, and not to judge the past, but to... find our way into the future.*
> - Douglas John Hall, *Thinking the Faith: Christian Theology in a North American Context* (Minneapolis: Augsburg, 1989), 28-29, 33, 36.

blinders / 20

"Nature, red in tooth and claw..."
- Alfred Tennyson, *In Memoriam*, Canto 56.

One of the most frequent objections to compassionate living in relation to diet has to do with the fact that animals kill and eat other animals. As animals ourselves, is it not reasonable for us to participate in this natural order of things? The simplest answer to that question is revealed in the asking of it – our capacity for reflection disqualifies us from unthinking entanglement in the law of "might makes right." But we must go further – there is a far greater ethical claim on us than anything suggested by our self-reflective cognitive skills alone.

Humans possess the remarkable ability to imagine ourselves into the joys and pains of other beings (J. M. Coetzee, *The Lives of Animals*, 34-35). Although for the most part we hold this empathic capacity in high esteem, we rarely embrace it without reservation once we have been personally exposed to the vulnerability and pain of it. But human history and individual experience remind us time and again of the great damage we do to ourselves and the grievous injustices we impose on others whenever we suppress empathy. This principle holds true whether we are steeling our hearts against the needs of other humans or against the agony of animals we wish to exploit.

We opted out of the "natural order of things" a long time ago, as we began fashioning weapons, cages, profits, and assembly-line massacre, revealing us to ourselves as a species with unique potential for unlimited malice and the matching power to use it. "Tooth and claw" is rarely cited as an ethical foundation for human behaviour, except as justification for our unhindered exploitation of other species. We desire, esteem and expect a kinder system of governance for ourselves, yet refuse to extend this favour to the most vulnerable among us. In so doing, we kill the very mercy that makes life sweet for any of us.

Humans generally take pride in being at the top of the food chain, in having won the war of "survival of the fittest." But we can no longer escape the "inconvenient" (Al Gore) and catastrophic truth that our apparent evolutionary success is decimating all other life on this planet, and threatening our own survival in the process. It is clear that the "long arc" (Martin Luther King Jr.) of survival requires from our species a different sort of "fitness" altogether. There are other survival principles at work in nature, as visceral as the mother/child bond, as democratic as the collective motion of flocks and schools and herds, and as altruistic as the protection and care of the weak.

Charles Darwin himself, great chronicler of the "struggle for existence," found in animals the ancient taproot of our goodness. In their instinct for "mutual aid," he saw the moral lineaments of human society. His writings are filled with admiring accounts of animal reciprocity, cooperation, and even love - a word, shunned by most evolutionary biologists, that appears some ninety-five times in the Descent of Man (against only two entries for survival of the fittest). Darwin beheld in even the humblest mammal the origins of the Golden Rule: Their "strong sexual, parental, and social instincts," he suggested, "give rise to 'do unto others as yourself' and 'love thy neighbor as thyself.'" Our ancestral line, contrary to the selfish gene reputation, has

given us a startling capacity to care deeply about what happens to each other.
- Marc Ian Barasch, *The Compassionate Life: Walking the Path of Kindness* (San Francisco: Berrett-Koehler Publishers, 2009), 19.

As reasoning creatures, we are capable of choosing the kind of relationship we want to have with the world. What would happen if, rather than defending our right to participate in the cruelty that we see in nature, we determined instead to emulate its reciprocity, cooperation and love, and to use our unique capabilities for the alleviation of suffering wherever we find it?

What if, rather than debating the upper limits of use and abuse permitted to us, we set our sights instead on those lower limits, on how our lives can be lived with the least possible imposition of suffering on others? It seems a modest proposal.

We, too, are under the law of necessity when – to prolong our own existence – we must bring other creatures to a painful end. But we should never cease to consider this as something tragic....Where we have a choice, we must avoid bringing torment and injury into the life of another, even the lowliest of creatures....Our own vocation is not to acquiesce in the cruelty of nature and even join in it, but rather to set a limit to it so far as our influence reaches.
- Albert Schweitzer, *The Animal World of Albert Schweitzer: Jungle Insights into Reverence for Life*, trans. and ed. Charles R. Joy (Boston: Beacon Press, 1950), 178-179.

limping / 21

I had snapped off the fruit from the tree of living things, and it could never be reattached.

We do not need to read the biblical creation story as literal history to appreciate the truths of our human experience that are depicted there: lost innocence, our universal complicity in all that is wrong in the world, and the curse of death. We do not need to believe the prophets when they speak of the coming of a better sort of world to recognize the one choice that will bring it closer for all of us: the simple decision to live as compassionately as possible.

I closed the book / 22

I took the veil in that moment and hid myself away, not from the eyes of the world, but from the pain of it.

Shutting out the pain of the world, at least to some degree, is an important survival mechanism for children. But carried through into adulthood, as it so often is, this practice becomes a deeply destructive force. We have no right to hide from the truth, particularly when we are the ones responsible for the suffering and when we have the means to ease it. So many people say that they "do not want to hear about it," that the reality is "too painful" for them. And then they continue making choices that inflict the very agony they can't even bear to think about.

the others / 23

That's as far as I can go.

This is what I believed, but it was not true. The truth is that I could have gone further if I had been willing to accept the pain of doing so. Since those early days of my awakening, I *have* gone further. I have watched babies being torn from their mothers' side to be killed. I have witnessed horrible deaths, and cruelties that left me trembling with anguish. Their suffering is our doing – we have no right to look away. Our contentment and ease of conscience are undeserved, purchased by illicit means, by detachment, concealment and denial.

To have integrity, to be whole, we need to look into the darkest corners of our proper responsibility and illuminate whatever truths we are concealing from ourselves. It is particularly unconscionable, and devastatingly harmful, to exclude from our awareness any suffering inflicted on others as a result of our choices.

blue skies / 24

I did not love them as a mother would, and that has become a great grief to my heart.

We loved our dogs, yet there were times when they felt lonely and afraid. They were part of the family, yet I did not try to see things through their eyes. Standing in for their mother, I understand now that I owed them more.

...no rest for the weary ones struggling to keep their footing.

Why was it a mechanical floor that finally tipped us off to the true nature of the university farm? Did that, of all things, reveal the no-heart of it all?

we lied / 26

We embraced the little orphan, cared for him tenderly, and then slit his throat.

We were not aware of what was being planned for the lamb, and it was years before we found out what had happened to him. But the truth is that we did not ask, we did not think, and in our cultivated ignorance, we betrayed him. In that baby's bewildered eyes, it did not make one bloody bit of difference which human held the knife – we all did.

mercy / 27

I need the rest of it, the soul of it, the geography of it – "with love."

> *He has showed you, O man, what is good.*
> *And what does the LORD require of you?*
> *To act justly and to love mercy*
> *and to walk humbly with your God.*
> - Micah 6:8 New International Version.
>
> *God is love.*
> - 1 John 4:16.

I recognize mercy in my husband's immediate response to end the bird's suffering, but I remain conflicted about such acts of "mercy-killing." I believe that only love can understand the delicate balance between justice and mercy, therefore love must be the heart and soul of all such hard choices. Love is the only guide capable of helping us navigate our way safely through the competing motivations and complex considerations of our lives. The more difficult the choice before us, the greater our need to humble ourselves before the gentle, but insistent, promptings of love.

In his book *Dominion,* Matthew Scully describes his "mercy-killing" of a little bird, and the love that opened his eyes, too late, to the possibility of a humbler choice:

*In the splatter I saw his little heart, and was horrified at the
bluntness of what I had done, obliterating this beautiful tiny
creature so finely made who tried so hard to live. At the time
my action seemed the only alternative, as it often does when
man brings his crushing force into an animal's world.*
- Matthew Scully, *Dominion: The Power of Man, the
Suffering of Animals, and the Call to Mercy* (New York:
St. Martin's Press, 2002), 4-5.

not really / 28

Do I want their hearts to break...?

Yes, let every human shield fail and every human heart shatter. That is
the only way for love to get in, or out, and for us to move beyond "not
really" into full awakening.

For those already trying to live with a broken-open heart, may my
words serve to give expression to your sorrow, and may our gathered
grief be a powerful force for the healing of the world.

without a thought / 29

It was only a spider.

> *If he is moved by the ethics of reverence for life, he injures and
> destroys life only under the compulsion of a necessity which he
> cannot escape, never from thoughtlessness.*
> - Albert Schweitzer, *The Animal World of Albert
> Schweitzer*, 174.

on the threshold / 30

...it is time to enter...

The memory of a vivid nightmare informs the imagery of this reflection.
Why enter a place of evil and danger, leaving behind a life of simple joys
and pleasures? In my dream I had no choice. In my waking that truth
remains.

Awakening

This section reflects on the stages of my conversion experience. As in any conversion, there are pivotal moments, flashes of recognition, sudden reversals of direction. But such dramatic transformations do not materialize out of thin air. They can be a lifetime in the making, emerging as they invariably do from a deeper life force, like long-anticipated blossoms flowering overnight on the branches of a maturing tree. And so, while this section is short, recounting those swift but decisive shifts brought about by a handful of critical experiences, it is the culmination of everything that came before. Though echoing the subject of this entire book (*A Chronicle of Awakening*), this particular chapter (*Awakening*) is an account, simply, of the opening of my eyes.

the end for me / 35

...I began to see...

I became a vegetarian in the spring of 2003 – at the age of 49 – during a sabbatical year in Europe. All my life I had been able to block from my mind the reality of what I was consuming. To do this, I needed to restrict my meat-eating to animals I had always eaten, whose flesh I was accustomed to thinking of as food on a plate. Animals I had not grown up eating – baby cows, horses, shrimp – I could not bear to eat because I had not learned to think of their flesh in this disconnected way.

In Europe, this dissociation is difficult to maintain. Birds are sold in markets with their heads and feet still attached, so that their identity can't be misrepresented. In France, a whole section of the supermarket is devoted to horsemeat. The flyer that I mention in my reflection depicted a pig looking towards the camera with a smiling expression, while its body was opened up to reveal where the various cuts of meat came from. I had seen similar information in pictorial charts before, but never with the animal's gaze directed towards the consumer, and never with the smile.

I was experiencing a disorienting onslaught of reality.

It was in Portugal that the last of my defences finally collapsed. We found ourselves stopped in traffic directly behind a truck, its back doors open and our eyes exposed to the rows of cows' bodies hanging there. In that one moment of painful illumination, I decided never to eat meat again.

All human life, we may say, consists solely of these two
activities: (1) bringing one's activities into harmony with
conscience, or (2) hiding from one's self the indications of
conscience in order to be able to continue to live as before.
- Leo Tolstoy, *Essays and Letters*, trans. Aylmer
Maude (London: Oxford University Press, 1911), 18.

Francois quote / 36

Twyla Francois, "Tara: The Story of One Sow," *Canadians for Ethical Treatment of Food Animals*, 2009.

what has the power? / 37

...happy families...playful babies...

Still in Portugal the day after becoming a vegetarian, I was taken to a specialty restaurant with baby pigs as the only main-course item on the menu. Larger-than-life murals covered the walls, depicting the various stages in the processing of those babies, from suckling at their mothers' sides, to metal skewers thrust through their tiny bodies, to presentation on serving platters. I was grateful for the decision I had made the day before, but horrified that people all around me were capable of eating those babies with obvious pleasure while surrounded by all that mother-grief and infant-suffering.

If I painted a building...

In the years that followed this initial moment of awakening, my awareness deepened and my distress swelled into agony over the treatment of animals at the hands of humans. I turned to art to try to express their suffering, and my grief. My art pieces were covered in strokes of black and red. And haunted by eyes.

When my son (the editor of this book) read this reflection and heard the story behind it, he created a painting – his first – and gave it to me as a gift. That painting forms the cover image of this book. Calvin intentionally followed the course of my experience, beginning with great broad strokes of black and red, and then covering them over with eyes.

The large eyes in the centre are mine. The blue throughout, the mingling of tears.

In the midst of a holocaust, how can art exist at all, other than for rescue's sake?

After writing these words, I rediscovered George Steiner's exploration of this subject. He suggests that the common notion of "art for art's sake" began as a "necessary rebellion against philistine didacticism and political control" but he warns against the potential for "pure narcissism" in such a view of art, and urges instead a return to the transformative vocation of "serious art":

> The indiscretion of serious art and literature and music is total. It queries the last privacies of our existence. This interrogation...is no abstract dialectic. It purposes change.... The waking, the enrichment, the complication, the darkening, the unsettling of sensibility and understanding which follow on our experience of art are incipient with action....In a wholly fundamental, pragmatic sense, the poem, the statue, the sonata are not so much read, viewed or heard as they are lived. The encounter with the aesthetic is, together with certain modes of religious and of metaphysical experience, the most "ingressive," transformative summons available to human experiencing....Such shifts are organically enfolded within categories of good and evil, of humane and inhumane conduct, of creative and destructive enactment.
> - George Steiner, *Real Presences* (Chicago: The University of Chicago Press, 1989), 142-143.

Is this what I have become, a messenger of ugliness and sadness, a thief of comfort, a prophet no one wants to hear?

So often now I find myself torn between keeping complicit silence or speaking unwelcome words, daily forced to choose between the comfortable rules of etiquette and the disturbing demands of suffering voices seeking to find passage through me.

Douglas John Hall speaks of this painful channelling of truth as the essence of the artistic experience. I believe it holds true for any of us who refuse to turn away from the needs of others:

> The artist "suffers," it is often said; and this can become an absurd romanticism if it is misunderstood....But if suffering is understood...as a consequence of allowing the subject a place within one's soul, or of failing to safeguard oneself against the subject; if it is understood, in short, as a kind of exposure of oneself to the raw stuff of existence - then perhaps this ancient

connection between art and suffering can be sustained. The
artist "suffers" the world to pass through him or her...
- Douglas John Hall, Thinking the Faith, 318.

What has the power to stop the horror.

I circle around this question all the time, both in this book and in my life. What had the power to change me, and what will inspire the shift in others, from blindness and distance to an awareness so immediate and overpowering that participation in the infliction of suffering becomes unthinkable? How and when does the change come?

Is it when we refuse to make peace with suffering, when we decide to become a "conscientious objector" to it (Calvin Neufeld, "A conscientious objector to suffering," *Geez*, Winter 2008, 42)?

Is it when we refuse to confine love, either within cages or within our own hardened hearts?

I have chosen to say, simply, that the change comes when we *see* the suffering. When we descend so deeply into seeing that our angle of vision shifts and we find ourselves looking out through the suffering eyes of others, experiencing their agony and terror as our own. The prelude to this awakening may take years, but there is often one moment – one particular suffering – that breaks something inside us and enters like a sword to pierce our own souls, letting truth rush in.

When that happens, will we try to find a way out for ourselves, will we struggle to find our own personal escape from the suffering, will we close our eyes and turn away? Or will we choose to prefer a broken heart over a faithless one, and do everything we can to rescue those we have begun to love?

Rolland quote / 38

[Christophe] could not think of the animals without shuddering in anguish. He looked into the eyes of the beasts and saw there a soul like his own, a soul which could not speak; but the eyes cried for it:
"What have I done to you? Why do you hurt me?"
He could not bear to see the most ordinary sights that he had seen hundreds of times – a calf crying in a wicker pen, with its big, protruding eyes, with their bluish whites and pink lids, and white lashes, its curly white tufts on its forehead, its purple snout, its knock-kneed legs: – a lamb being carried by a peasant with its four legs tied together, hanging head down,

trying to hold its head up, moaning like a child, bleating and lolling its gray tongue: – fowls huddled together in a basket: – the distant squeals of a pig being bled to death: – a fish being cleaned on the kitchen-table....The nameless tortures which men inflict on such innocent creatures made his heart ache. Grant animals a ray of reason, imagine what a frightful nightmare the world is to them: a dream of cold-blooded men, blind and deaf, cutting their throats, slitting them open, gutting them, cutting them into pieces, cooking them alive, sometimes laughing at them and their contortions as they writhe in agony....To a man whose mind is free there is something even more intolerable in the sufferings of animals than in the sufferings of men. For with the latter it is at least admitted that suffering is evil and that the man who causes it is a criminal. But thousands of animals are uselessly butchered every day without a shadow of remorse. If any man were to refer to it, he would be thought ridiculous.
  - Romain Rolland, "The Burning Bush," in *Jean-Christophe: Journey's End*, trans. Gilbert Cannan (New York: Henry Holt and Company, 1913), 327-328.

Horribly, "thousands" is nowhere near the number of animals "uselessly butchered every day":

Every day, we cause over thirty million birds and mammals and forty-five million fish to be fatally attacked so we can eat them, and it's universally considered to be good food for good people. With these meals, we feed our shadow, which grows strong and bold as it gorges itself on our repressed grief, guilt, and revulsion.
  - Will Tuttle, "Feeding the shadow self," *The World Peace Diet* blog, 19 January 2012.

who will speak? / 39

I forced myself to keep watching, not to turn away, not to close my eyes, not to protect myself.

In the summer of 2007 I watched *Chew On This*, a film produced by People for the Ethical Treatment of Animals (PETA). All I remember now is that one pig. I wanted so desperately to look away from the torture she endured. But her helpless agony took me that one step further towards awakening, and I realized at that moment that I could no longer contribute in any way to an animal industry that included, protected, even spawned, such abuses. Within a few months I had transitioned permanently from a vegetarian to a vegan diet. In the years since then, I have become aware of the abuses routinely endured by egg-laying hens and by lactating cows, and of the cruel requirements of a heartless system that has no use for male infants, no tolerance for natural motherhood, and no mercy for the mother/child bond. I used to consider it sufficient to give up eating "anything that had to die," but I now know that eggs and dairy products contain just as much death, suffering and grief as do those bleeding packages of body parts.

...given what is happening to them, why does it matter one bit what becomes of me?

One theme that recurs often in these reflections is my visceral sense that my own suffering is *nothing* compared to theirs, and that therefore my own suffering in response to their pain does not matter. I know that I am not alone in having these feelings. Here I choose to affirm that vicarious human trauma experienced in response to animal suffering matters deeply.

It matters, because if I can no longer go on, then who will speak for them?

I have found it extraordinarily hard, in the face of the suffering I have witnessed, to attach any importance to what becomes of me, other than this mission of mine to ease that suffering. For a long time it was a matter of resolve for me to affirm more than this, but I do so now with all the conviction of imperative truth: each life matters, in and of itself. We cannot build a happier, more compassionate world while excluding anyone from it, even ourselves.

Tennyson and Stevenson quotes / 40

Alfred Tennyson, *In Memoriam*, Canto 54.

Robert Louis Stevenson, quoted in *The Extended Circle: A Dictionary of Humane Thought*, comp. Jon Wynne-Tyson (Fontwell, Sussex: Centaur Press, 1985), 355.

I wish to God / 41

I saw and I heard and I wished to God I had not.

I wished to God I had not seen those brutalized bodies hanging from hooks in the back of a truck. *I wished to God* I had not heard pigs crying in the heat at a rest stop. *I wished to God* I had not looked into the eyes of that cow staring into mine as I traveled behind.
But I did see and I did hear and I did look, and it did change me. Now I wish to God for something entirely different. Not for my own escape from awareness, not for my own wilful ignorance, but rather for a way out of their suffering and out of my complicity. *I wish to God* for rescue.

Walker quote / 42

> *...to think there are people who do not know that animals suffer. People like me who have forgotten, and daily forget, all that animals try to tell us....We are used to drinking milk from containers showing "contented" cows, whose real lives we want to hear nothing about, eating eggs and drumsticks from "happy" hens, and munching hamburgers advertised by bulls of integrity who seem to command their fate.*
>
> *As we talked of freedom and justice one day for all, we sat down to steaks. I am eating misery, I thought, as I took the first bite. And spit it out.*
>
> - Alice Walker, "Am I Blue?" in *The McGraw-Hill Reader: Issues Across the Disciplines*, 11th ed., ed. Gilbert H. Muller (Boston: McGraw-Hill, 2011), 759-760.

my story / 43

It is like there is a crack in the world...

Originally published in *The Peaceable Table*, December 2010.

...playful babies who don't know how little time they have...

I called them "babies." The following chart shows just how accurate that term is. Compiled by Colleen Patrick-Goudreau (The Compassionate Cook) using data from the United States Department of Agriculture (USDA). Abridged and used by permission.

An Unnatural Life Span

Slaughtering animals when they are babies is standard, whether they are raised conventionally or in operations that are labeled "humane," "sustainable," "natural," "free-range," "cage-free," "heritage-bred," "grass-fed," "local," or "organic."

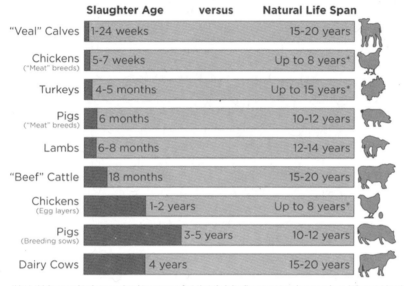

	Slaughter Age	versus	Natural Life Span	
"Veal" Calves	1-24 weeks		15-20 years	
Chickens ("Meat" breeds)	5-7 weeks		Up to 8 years*	
Turkeys	4-5 months		Up to 15 years*	
Pigs ("Meat" breeds)	6 months		10-12 years	
Lambs	6-8 months		12-14 years	
"Beef" Cattle	18 months		15-20 years	
Chickens (Egg layers)	1-2 years		Up to 8 years*	
Pigs (Breeding sows)	3-5 years		10-12 years	
Dairy Cows	4 years		15-20 years	

*Most chickens and turkeys are bred to grow so fast that their bodies cannot endure very long. When not bred for consumption, chickens and turkeys can grow at a rate that their bodies can sustain for many years.

www.CompassionateCook.com

Jesus quote / 44

Matthew 20:22 International Standard Version.

the cup / 45

Luke 22:39-46 Good News Bible.

What is the temptation?

As Jesus was experiencing his great agony in the Garden of Gethsemane (at the foot of the Mount of Olives) prior to his arrest and crucifixion, his disciples escaped from their grief by falling into a deep sleep. This is what I tried to do for a long time. I turned away from the suffering ones because the pain of thinking about them seemed too much for me to bear.

I let myself "retreat to the convenience of being overwhelmed" (David Rakoff, "Richard Ford, Remembering David Rakoff," *The Next Chapter*, CBC Radio, 17 September 2012).

The temptation is always with us. So many ways to run away from grief.

Witness

Years ago, I dreamt that I held in my arms a mute child who had been terribly hurt. She needed me to help her find her voice so that she could reveal what had happened to her, because then she could be well again. That dream has become my life.

Images of suffering and narratives of cruelty break through and claim me now, hanging about my neck, begging for a voice. Truth carries with it its own necessities, its own inexorability. I have been left with no choice but to bear *witness* to the truth, to make it *known* (Sanskrit "vid") and to make it *seen* (Latin "videre"). A vocation of witness, for the sake of rescue and healing. A vocation with a claim on every one of us.

beginning somewhere / 49

I now have no way back to my personal garden of innocence and comfort without bringing them with me.

Eden and Gethsemane, two gardens framing the biblical narrative, the first a mythic paradise from which our guilt expelled us, the second a gnarled olive grove where Jesus wept for a hurting world. The only return to happiness and wellbeing for any of us is to sweat those drops of grief for the healing of the world. There is no individual return. Only love can bring us back, and love leaves no one behind.

On Easter Sunday 2012, I walked through an interactive church installation commemorating the final hours of Jesus' life. At the station representing the Garden of Gethsemane, we were invited to write a personal response to Jesus' call to his sleeping disciples: "Wake up!"

My response: "I'm awake now. I can't sleep. God help me!"

A few days later I received information about horrific conditions at an egg-laying facility in Pennsylvania (Christian Vegetarian Association newsletter, 13 April 2012). It was many months before I could bring myself to follow the links to the article and video, but that day I was undone by one line in the newsletter itself: "decapitated by an automatic feeding cart."

Frantic with anguish, desperate for someone to tell, I started a blog and began that day to bear witness. I reached for a name that would do justice to the enormity of everything that had been pressing so painfully against my heart. I chose the name "Suffering Eyes" and, "beginning somewhere," began here. The blog would later form the foundation of the first part of this book.

Richter quote / 50

> *He sins against life when he separates them as though they were but machinery....Is the heart, beating under bristles, feathers, or hard wing-covers, therefore any the less a heart?*
> - Jean Paul Friedrich Richter, *Levana, or The Doctrine of Education*, trans. Anne Holt (London: G. Bell & Sons, 1913), 342.

the lucky ones / 51

Just to be absolutely clear: in no way do I consider those infant victims to be "lucky." In writing this reflection, I found myself overwhelmed by the thought of the protracted sufferings awaiting their siblings. What hell is it where being ground alive as a newborn is preferable to the alternative?

That evil world where cold eyes look and pick and sort, and all the little boy bodies drop into grinders.

There is a brutality of evil, of sadistic pleasure and violent rage unleashed on defenceless victims. The undercover videos leave me trembling with agony and with my own helpless rage. But there is also a coldness of evil, of impenetrable walls, cold steel, routine procedures, and deadened hearts:

> *Sin is for one man to walk brutally over the life of another and to be quite oblivious of the wounds he has left behind.*
> - Shusaku Endo, *Silence*, trans. William Johnston (New York: Taplinger, 1979), 132.

Holocaust survivor Elie Wiesel relates a haunting encounter he had with this absence of empathy, while he and his family awaited transportation to a concentration camp:

My parents and I stood close to the fence: on the other side were life and liberty, or what men call life and liberty. A few passers-by; they averted their faces; the more sensitive bowed their heads. It was then that I saw him, a face in the window across the way. The curtains hid the rest of him; only his head was visible. It was like a balloon. Bald, flat nose, wide empty eyes. A bland face, banal, bored: no passion ruffled it. I watched it for a long time. It was gazing out, reflecting no pity, no pleasure, no shock, not even anger or interest. Impassive, cold, impersonal.
      - Elie Wiesel, *The Town Beyond the Wall* (New York: Schocken Books, 1982), 150.

Reflecting later on this passage, Elie Wiesel commented:

It is then that I actually began thinking of the dangers, of the perils of indifference, which has motivated my activities for years and years and years. I came to the conclusion then...that the opposite of love is not hate but indifference....The opposite of life is not death but indifference. It is because of that face that I remember. The face in the window.
      - Elie Wiesel, "An Evening with Elie Wiesel," University of California Santa Barbara, *Herman P. and Sophia Taubman Endowed Symposia in Jewish Studies,* 19 August 2002.

We have all been that face in the window, dead to the needs of others. It is a fearful thing to look into suffering eyes and recognize their rightful claim on us. And so we do not allow their wounds a place in our souls, we anaesthetize our hearts, we hollow them out. What begins as an effort to protect ourselves from pain and risk soon swells into a numbing of all self-awareness, because how can we bear the knowledge of what we have become?

What we don't realize is that if we stand at that window long enough, there will be nothing left of us.

The great enemy of morality has always been indifference.... Many people become like houses in which one story after another has been vacated, a lifeless structure in which all windows look empty and strange, deserted.
      - Albert Schweitzer, *The Words of Albert Schweitzer,* ed. Norman Cousins (New York: Newmarket Press, 1984), 61.

We may remain insensible to what we have lost, but others will feel the weight of it.

> *I shall strike you without anger*
> *And without hate, like a butcher.*
> - Charles Baudelaire, *The Flowers of Evil,* quoted in *Creaturely Poetics: Animality and Vulnerability in Literature and Film,* by Anat Pick (New York: Columbia University Press, 2011), 139.

> *In the best of times, it is but by flashes, when our whole nature is clear, strong, and conscious...that we enjoy communion with our soul. At the worst, we are so fallen and passive that we may say shortly we have none....Consciousness becomes engrossed among the reflex and mechanical parts of life, and soon loses both the will and power to look higher considerations in the face. This is ruin; this is the last failure in life....What shall it profit a man if he gain the whole world and lose himself?'*
> - Robert Louis Stevenson, *Ethical Studies* (London: W. Heinemann, 1924), 28-29.

A simple protest...

Malcolm Muggeridge gave up eating meat in order to be "free to denounce those horrible factory farms" (reported by Marian Burros, "In Defense of Vegetarianism: Seven Yeas," *The New York Times,* 13 October 1982).

> *One can scarcely look for the Good Shepherd in factory farms, where animals are accorded just enough room to stand up in; where they never see the light of the sun, or the green of the grass, or the blue of the sky.*
> - Malcolm Muggeridge, *The Very Best of Malcolm Muggeridge,* ed. Ian A. Hunter (Vancouver: Regent College Publishing, 2003), 226.

A simple proposal: if everyone who is troubled by the horrors of factory farming and assembly-line slaughter were to follow Muggeridge's example and discontinue their financial support of the animal industry, their protest would exert enormous pressure on these companies to improve the appalling profit-driven conditions under which animals are being legally tortured.

And perhaps, in the process, these protesters would experience the freedom of living as compassionately as possible, and would awaken to the brutality – and immorality – involved in all unnecessary killing.

Inge quote / 52

> It is...an unproved assumption that the domination of the planet by our own species is a desirable thing, which must give satisfaction to its Creator. We have devastated the loveliness of the world; we have exterminated several species more beautiful and less vicious than ourselves; we have enslaved the rest of the animal creation, and have treated our distant cousins in fur and feathers so badly that beyond doubt, if they were able to formulate a religion, they would depict the Devil in human form.
> - William Ralph Inge, *Outspoken Essays, Second Series* (London: Longmans, Green and Co., 1922), 166-167.

who are we? / 53

This is who we are.

The film I watched is called *10 Billion Lives*, because that is the number of animals killed for food each year in the United States alone. Those who choose to look away, as I did for most of my life, must on some level recognize this simple truth:

> *No one must...regard as non-existent the sufferings of which he spares himself the sight.*
> - Albert Schweitzer, *Civilization and Ethics, The Philosophy of Civilization, Part II,* 2nd ed., trans. C. T. Campion (London: A. & C. Black, 1929), 257.

I write in the belief that most people who allow themselves to look at suffering will be moved to end their participation in its infliction. But knowledge alone is not enough. There are those who may visit slaughterhouses, watch documentaries about factory farms, and read accounts of infant trust betrayed; they may even hold the knife in their own hands, and watch the life drain from helpless eyes looking up at them; and still the armour surrounding their hearts may remain intact.

If I could understand the roots of such entrenched indifference, could I find words to tear it down?

But there are no such words, and I have no such power.

Instead, I offer these words of my awareness and grief, in the hope that they will cultivate living tendrils of kindness and sorrow, capable of crumbling a mountain of apathy.

the snake / 54

I have heard allegations - and confessions - of this deliberately done.

I have heard people confess to deliberately killing any snake they come across. They justify their action by their fear. This in a country (Canada) where there are virtually no dangerous snakes at all.

I regularly stop my car to move turtles off the road. One day I was having difficulty nudging a particularly large snapping turtle to safety. A park ranger who stopped to help told me that some people deliberately swerve to hit them.

feeble / 55

...ripping apart great beautiful beings and leaving the babies to die of grief.

The documentary I watched was *For the Love of Elephants: The Nature of Things with David Suzuki* (CBC, 25 August 2010). It is described as an "intimate portrait of the elephant-human bond that is formed in an elephant rehabilitation centre just outside Nairobi, Kenya." Horrible as it is that mature elephants are killed for their tusks, what I was not prepared for was the sight of the babies, their little trunks desperately caressing the bodies of their dead and dying mothers, hopeless baby eyes looking wildly out into the world not knowing what to do or where to go. And the rescued baby, dehydrated, grief-stricken, crying, traumatized, exhausted, pacing and refusing to sleep until she finally collapses to the floor.

And the others, the ones who don't survive despite the day-and-night efforts of the keepers, dying because their emotional pain has taken from them the will to live.

> *I think they cry because they can remember what happened to their mother...*
> - Mishak Nzimi, in *For the Love of Elephants.*

the day I broke / 56

It was more than a million. The reason doesn't matter.

Jesus quote / 58

"Whatever you did to them, you did to me."

> *Truly I tell you, whatever you did for one of the least of these*
> *brothers and sisters of mine, you did for me....Whatever you*
> *did not do for one of the least of these, you did not do for me.*
> - Jesus, Matthew 25: 40, 45 NIV.

I hear these words as the truth of anyone who loves.

your torment / 59

Down on the floor with my screams, trying to block out theirs...

In the face of their torment, my concern for my own emotional wellbeing feels to me like an obscenity. And my words worse than silence.

Endo quote / 60

Priest's cry in *Silence,* by Shusaku Endo, 141.

despair / 61

Like those tragic figures in an ancient painting...

This reflection recalls an illustration from my childhood Bible depicting the story of Noah's ark. I remember as a child being troubled by that picture, but my faith community's frame of reference gradually superimposed itself over my simple perception of it. I learned to overlook the foreground horror of mothers clutching babies, begging for mercy, reaching out in despair towards an ark firmly locked against them. I learned to look at that painting without seeing the truth of it. Now I see the cold cruelty of those rising waters, the heartless exclusivity of that closed ark, and the meaninglessness of a rainbow that withholds its promise from those most in need of it.

I ask myself how it is possible that I did not see this before. What twisted ideology closed my eyes to the truth? The same distortions continue to this day, in arks of protection and rainbows of promise meant only for humans. And an ocean of indifference swallowing the lives of the ones left out.

traditional prayer / 62

Traditional prayer, in *A Child's Good Night Book,* by Margaret Wise Brown (New York: William R. Scott, Inc., 1943), final page (unnumbered). Adapted for use on back cover.

sanctuary / 63

...two human beings with loving hearts and a rescue mission.

It is commonly believed that the alleviation of human suffering ought to be our highest priority, that the wellbeing of animals matters less than our own. In the hierarchy of caring, how can we justify spending limited human resources on rescuing a handful of baby rabbits, or investing emotional energy, as I have done this week, in the plight of mother sheep bleating for their stolen babies?

Charities serving human needs compete with one another for resources, yet they respect one another's work. The concerns of animal welfare advocates, however, are regularly dismissed with a handful of passionate words declaring in no uncertain terms: "Well, *I* care about people! How can you concern yourself with animals, when there is so much human suffering in the world?" This reasoning is fundamentally flawed, setting up a false dichotomy between supposedly competing interests, as if one arena of caring is capable of detracting from another. The truth is quite the reverse: the more expansive our circle of caring, the greater our capacity for compassion.

The attitude that human suffering of any kind has a higher priority on our attention than animal suffering, however severe, can only be explained by the entrenched prejudice of "speciesism." We human animals have decided that our own interests are the only ones that really matter, to the exclusion of the claims of all other species. The roots of this prejudice are so entangled in our beliefs, attitudes, institutions and practices, that most of us cannot imagine a worldview existing outside of it.

Surely it is unthinkable to suggest that all human misery must be brought to an end before we can tend to the needs of anyone else. A more just triage of priorities could be achieved if the following criteria were taken into consideration: the magnitude and severity of the need; personal responsibility for the existence of that need in the first place; individual ability to do something to alleviate it; and the inability of those in need to help themselves.

In relation to all these criteria, animals have an overwhelming claim on every human being's priorities. The magnitude of the need is unparalleled: billions of animals living and dying in agony. Personal responsibility for the need is inescapable: they suffer and die as a direct consequence of our choices. The ability to alleviate the need is uncomplicated: we can stop demanding their slaughter. And the powerlessness of animals to defend themselves against our abuse of power is undeniable, and complete.

One final thought. Working to alleviate animal suffering, providing sanctuaries of rescue and healing for them – this is not charity. The ongoing history of our abusive relationship with animals has left us with a debt we can never repay, and a guilt for which we can never atone. Anything we do for them is less than they deserve from us, and less than we owe.

Cohen lyrics / 64

O gather up the brokenness
And bring it to me now
The fragrance of those promises
You never dared to vow

The splinters that you carry
The cross you left behind
Come healing of the body
Come healing of the mind

And let the heavens hear it
The penitential hymn
Come healing of the spirit
Come healing of the limb

Behold the gates of mercy
In arbitrary space
And none of us deserving
The cruelty or the grace

O solitude of longing
Where love has been confined
Come healing of the body
Come healing of the mind

O see the darkness yielding
That tore the light apart
Come healing of the reason
Come healing of the heart

O troubled dust concealing
An undivided love
The Heart beneath is teaching
To the broken heart above

O let the heavens falter
And let the earth proclaim:
Come healing of the Altar
Come healing of the Name

O longing of the branches
To lift the little bud
O longing of the arteries
To purify the blood

And let the heavens hear it
The penitential hymn
Come healing of the spirit
Come healing of the limb

O let the heavens hear it
The penitential hymn
Come healing of the spirit
Come healing of the limb

I remember you / 65

Gathering sorrows like sheaves...

Are these our only options – to bury our awareness or to be buried by it? Either we perpetuate the suffering by trying to forget it, or we remember the suffering ones, take their suffering into ourselves, and experience with them the desperate urgency to end it.

I remember the circus elephant, struck by a train while waiting to board. *I remember* the horse forced off a cliff for a movie stunt, the puppy tossed off a cliff by a laughing soldier. *I remember* the dogs, crammed into cages in blistering heat and thirst, tin cans shoved over their noses, their legs dislocated and tied behind their backs, waiting to be slaughtered. *I remember* the moon bears, strapped down immobile for years, painful catheters continuously extracting their bile. *I remember* the turkeys and pigs and cows and calves, beaten, broken, tortured.

And *I remember* the cow looking out the back of the truck, directly into my eyes, her hopelessness meeting my helplessness.

> *Only at quite rare moments have I felt really glad to be alive. I could not but feel with a sympathy full of regret all the pain that I saw around me, not only that of men but that of the whole creation. From this community of suffering I have never tried to withdraw myself. It seemed to me a matter of course that we should all take our share of the burden of pain which lies upon the world....But however much concerned I was at the problem of the misery in the world, I never let myself get lost in broodings over it; I always held firmly to the thought that each one of us can do a little to bring some portion of it to an end.*
> *- Albert Schweitzer, My Life and Thought, trans. C. T. Campion (London: Allen & Unwin, 1933), 279-280.*

Hindi quote / 66

> *We were told that fish had no feelings, and we killed them with abandon....Carp typically were left to suffocate on the shore.... Sometimes I would give a fleeting thought to whether these animals suffered as they lay gasping on the shore....Once we brought M-80 firecrackers to the lake. We stuffed one into the gill of a large carp, lit the waterproof fuse, and released him. Seconds later the water erupted in a red spray. When the muddy water cleared, we saw the carp's head, blasted away*

from his body. I watched tentacles of flesh sway back and forth in the current. Small fish inspected them with curiosity. For some reason we felt bad about this, although no one said anything in particular. We did not do that again. Looking back at it, however, I guess that victim suffered far less than those who suffocated.
- Steve Hindi, "I Was a Killer," in *The Missing Peace: The Hidden Power of Our Kinship with Animals,* ed. Tina Volpe and Judy Carman (Flourtown, PA: Dreamriver Press, 2009), 94-95.

gasping / 67

...gasping mouths unable to process the oxygen surrounding them like a grave.

Former hunter and angler Steve Hindi, founder of Showing Animals Respect and Kindness (SHARK), tells of one fish – a 20-pound baby Mako shark – which made a particularly unsettling impression on him. He left the shark to die by suffocation so that the body would be in perfect condition for mounting. This is Hindi's account of the baby's slow death:

> *I don't remember how long it took him to die, but it was very long. Every now and then I would open the hatch to see if he was dead yet, and he would look at me. Sharks can move their eyes to a point, and they can and do follow activities around them. I will never forget that baby watching me as I waited for him to die. This was probably the lowest I dropped in my long history of killing.*
> - Steve Hindi, "I Was a Killer," 99.

Hindi remembers being brought up as a child to care about animal welfare, but to disregard the suffering of fish. He was taught that fish do not suffer. He describes the gradual shift that took place in his experience of fishing, great enjoyment giving way before growing uneasiness. Eventually what he was left with was grief, with a "debt I could never repay," and he buried his "trophy" victims "next to the graves of beloved nonhuman family members" (101).

Like Hindi, our children are taught to make a sport of tormenting and killing fish, or tormenting them and releasing them wounded. We teach them to consider this a pleasure. This is a serious breach of our responsibility to guide our children towards compassion. Rather, we are modelling the suppression of empathy.

Considered by magnitude alone, the suffering caused by commercial fisheries is beyond all imagining, statistics counted by billions of individuals, by kilometres of fishing lines, by tonnes per catch. Jonathan Safran Foer cites researchers at the Fisheries Centre of the University of British Columbia who describe modern fishing practices as "wars of extermination." Foer goes on to say:

> War *is precisely the right word to describe our relationship to fish – it captures the technologies and techniques brought to bear against them, and the spirit of domination.*
> - Jonathan Safran Foer, *Eating Animals* (New York: Back Bay Books, 2009), 33.

Individual suffering is too often concealed by numbers and statistics, by broad views that cannot bring the focus close enough. Foer draws our eyes nearer, helps us to see commercial fishing from the perspective of its victims:

> *In trawlers, hundreds of different species are crushed together, gashed on corals, bashed on rocks – for hours – and then hauled from the water, causing painful decompression (the decompression sometimes causes the animals' eyes to pop out or their internal organs to come out their mouths)....Most of these sea animals, though, die on the ship itself, where they will slowly suffocate or have their gills cut while conscious. In some cases, the fish are tossed onto ice, which can actually prolong their deaths....No fish gets a good death. Not a single one. You never have to wonder if the fish on your plate had to suffer. It did.*
> - Jonathan Safran Foer, *Eating Animals*, 192-193.

Voltaire quote / 68

> *It is in my opinion giving up the light of reason, to pretend to assert, that beasts are no more than mere machines; for, is it not a manifest contradiction, to acknowledge that God has given them the organs of sense, and then to affirm that they have no sense?*
>
> *Besides, I think one must never have made any observation upon animals, not to distinguish in them the different cries of want, suffering, joy, fear, love, anger, and indeed all other affections of the mind or body; surely, it would*

be very strange, that they should so well express what they
have no sense of!
  - Voltaire, A *Treatise upon Toleration* (Glasgow:
  printed for Robert Urie, 1765), 90.

The fact that Voltaire needed to affirm the sentience of other species, points an accusing finger at the treacherous insensitivity that has characterized so much religious dogma and philosophical rationalism in human history. The chasm that is supposed to exist between us and all other life forms has been chiselled out by humans with tragic results for everyone, ourselves included. In casting animals continuously into the pit of cruelty and indifference that has opened up along that fault line, we cannot help but be swallowed up by it ourselves.

It has often been this self-interest, this concern over how the contagion of cruelty and indifference infects our dealings with each other, which has motivated appeals for the "humane" treatment of animals. Eighteenth-century philosopher Immanuel Kant constructed a roundabout argument for kindness towards animals, but astonishingly attempted to do so without conceding to them any intrinsic value:

> *But so far as animals are concerned we have no direct duties.*
> *Animals are not self-conscious and are there merely as a*
> *means to an end. That end is man....Our duties towards*
> *animals are merely indirect duties towards humanity....If he is*
> *not to stifle his human feelings, he must practice kindness*
> *towards animals, for he who is cruel to animals becomes hard*
> *also in his dealing with men. We can judge the heart of a man*
> *by his treatment of animals....Tender feelings towards dumb*
> *animals develop humane feelings towards mankind....Our*
> *duties towards animals, then, are indirect duties towards*
> *mankind.*
>   - Immanuel Kant, "Duties to Animals," in
>   *Environmental Ethics: Divergence and Convergence*, 2nd
>   ed., ed. Richard G. Botzler and Susan J. Armstrong
>   (Boston: McGraw Hill, 1998), 312-313.

It would be shocking to hear anyone articulate such blatant anthropocentrism today, but Kant's words embody the practical philosophy undergirding every aspect of our use of animals. Rejecting that philosophy would mean rethinking everything we are doing to them. And it would expose us as we are, not as the glorified pinnacle of creation, but rather as violent thieves and oppressors.

These words are not exaggerated or defamatory. On the contrary, the commonplace human treatment of animals from ancient times to the present reveals this assessment as accurate and deserved.

As for the argument that religious faith justifies (or even requires) a view of animals as created for the purpose of human exploitation and domination, such an attitude forgets (or ignores) the Edenic ideal of humans as caretakers of other species, not as self-centred users and abusers of them.

heart of darkness / 69

"Turkey-bowling," they called it....this desecration, this reduction of bodies that used to be beautiful...

Was it not enough that their lives were stolen from them, must their bodies then become objects of amusement, of entertainment, of human *pleasure?* Like the calves and goats whose heads and feet are cut off, their torsos tossed about by riders on horseback in Buzkashi, the national sport of Afghanistan. Like all creatures whose lingering tortures and gruesome deaths feed perverted human pleasures – the bulls, the dogs, the foxes, the birds, the fish.

A defenceless creature's whole world ripped apart, for a game.

Shaw and MacDonald quotes / 70

"If you cannot attain to knowledge without torturing a dog, you must do without knowledge."

When a man says to Society, "May I torture my mother in pursuit of knowledge?" Society replies, "No." If he pleads, "What! Not even if I have a chance of finding out how to cure cancer by doing it?" Society still says, "Not even then." If the scientist, making the best of his disappointment, goes on to ask may he torture a dog, the stupid and callous people who do not realize that a dog is a fellow-creature and sometimes a good friend, may say Yes....But even those who say "You may torture A dog" never say "You may torture MY dog." And nobody says, "Yes, because in the pursuit of knowledge you may do as you please." Just as even the stupidest people say, in effect, "If you cannot attain to knowledge without burning your mother you must do without knowledge," so the wisest people say, "If you

cannot attain to knowledge without torturing a dog, you must do without knowledge."
- George Bernard Shaw, *The Doctor's Dilemma: Preface on Doctors*, 1909 (gutenberg.org).

"...whose little treasure we would tear from them in order to add to our own wealth..."

These words are selected and paraphrased from a sermon preached by Thomas Wingfold, a character in an 1870 novel by George MacDonald. The sermon was later reprinted in an anti-vivisectionist pamphlet.

Can it be right to water the tree of knowledge with blood, and stir its boughs with the gusts of bitter agony, that we may force its flowers into blossom before their time?...Will it justify the same as a noble, a laudable, a worshipful endeavor to cover it with the reason or pretext – God knows which – of such love for my own human kind as strengthens me to the most ruthless torture of their poorer relations, whose little treasure I would tear from them that it may teach me how to add to [our] wealth? May my God give me grace to prefer a hundred deaths to a life gained by the suffering of one simplest creature....God in Heaven! who, what is the man who would dare live a life wrung from the agonies of tortured innocents?
- George MacDonald, *Paul Faber, Surgeon* (New York: George Routledge & Sons, 1900), 177.

The sordid history of vivisection is drenched with accounts of torture, with horrors beyond belief. Regulatory agencies now set limits to what may be done to animals in pursuit of scientific knowledge, but even within those parameters, researchers are still permitted to inflict discomfort, distress, confinement, loneliness, fear, pain and death. How will future generations look back on our present actions? Perhaps it will be with the same revulsion that we presently feel towards scientists who dissected dogs without anaesthetics, or who conducted maternal deprivation and total isolation experiments on infant monkeys, driving them to insanity.

I was particularly struck by the change of heart experienced by Michael Allen Fox. In his "Animal Experimentation: A Philosopher's Changing Views" (1987), he repudiated the central arguments of his earlier *The Case for Animal Experimentation* (1986). He identified a major flaw in his previous views: they had been based on philosophical abstractions that omitted the legitimate role of feeling in the development of ethical understanding. Factoring the emotional element into his consideration of moral principles led him to the discovery of a deeper ethic:

> *The new Fox draws our attention to the harm-avoidance principle, or "principle of non-maleficence," which says that we have an obligation to avoid harming the innocent. He now rejects the idea that experimentation that harms animals is justified if the benefits to humans (and/or other animals) "outweigh" the harm done to the animals experimented upon. Those scientists and others who accept this cost/benefit approach, he says, ignore the deeper question of whether it is morally acceptable to benefit from the harms we cause to other beings. In other words, to show that we would be worse off if we stopped animal experimentation is not to resolve the moral issue.*
> - Angus Taylor, *Animals and Ethics: An Overview of the Philosophical Debate* (Toronto: Broadview Press, 2003), 130-131.

the beast below / 71

Doctor Who, "The Beast Below," BBC, 10 April 2010.

...an account of torture...

The lecture I attended took place in June 2010. In searching for the study the speaker was citing, I was disturbed to discover the sheer number of similar studies, repeating (with variations) the same sort of experiments. This particular test involved seven sleep-deprived rats:

> *Three deprived rats died after 5, 13, and 33 days while being observed....Four deprived rats were killed...after 5, 13, 19, and 21 days, because death seemed imminent....Obvious pathological signs in deprived rats included: fluid in lungs and trachea...collapsed lung...internal hemorrhage...severe edema in limbs...testicles atrophied...severe scrotal damage...and much-enlarged bladder....These results support the view that sleep does serve a vital physiological function.*
> - Allan Rechtschaffen et al., "Physiological Correlates of Prolonged Sleep Deprivation in Rats," *Science* 221 (July 1983): 182-184.

...the never-ending screams and whimpers of our weaker cousins...

> *The so-called lower animals are literally our distant cousins.*
> *They have as good a right on this planet as we have; they were*
> *not made for our benefit as we used to suppose.*
> - William Ralph Inge, *Outspoken Essays*, 56.

As animals sharing this planet with our non-human relations, we can recognize in them our intrinsic family connection. Yet the discernible distance between us and these "distant cousins" of ours denies us the right to judge them (and in so doing to find them deficient) by standards that we choose as normative:

> *We patronize them for their incompleteness, for their tragic*
> *fate of having taken form so far below ourselves. And therein*
> *do we err. For the animal shall not be measured by man. In a*
> *world older and more complete than ours they move finished*
> *and complete, gifted with extensions of the senses we have lost*
> *or never attained, living by voices we shall never hear. They*
> *are not brethren, they are not underlings; they are other*
> *nations, caught with ourselves in the net of life and time,*
> *fellow-prisoners of the splendour and travail of the earth.*
> - Henry Beston, *The Outermost House* (London: Selwyn & Blount, 1928), 39-40.

This episode of *Doctor Who* is but one example of the imagination's potential to provide moral leadership. Nonviolence towards animals is central to a wide range of hopeful visions for the future:

> *They will neither harm nor destroy on all my holy mountain...*
> - Isaiah 11:9.

> *I have no doubt that it is a part of the destiny of the human*
> *race, in its gradual improvement, to leave off eating animals...*
> - Henry David Thoreau, *Walden and Civil Disobedience* (New York: W. W. Norton & Company, 1966), 144.

> *The day may come, when the rest of the animal creation may*
> *acquire those rights which never could have been withholden*
> *from them but by the hand of tyranny.*
> - Jeremy Bentham, *An Introduction to the Principles of Morals and Legislation*, ed. J. H. Burns and H. L. A. Hart (London: Athlone Press, 1970), 283n.

Very little of the great cruelty shown by men can really be attributed to cruel instinct. Most of it comes from thoughtlessness or inherited habit. The roots of cruelty, therefore, are not so much strong as widespread. But the time must come when inhumanity protected by custom and thoughtlessness will succumb before humanity championed by thought.
Let us work that this time may come.
- Albert Schweitzer, *The Animal World of Albert Schweitzer*, 179.

We no longer enslave animals for food purposes.
- William T. Riker, *Star Trek: The Next Generation*, "Lonely Among Us," 2 November 1987.

What you're doing isn't self-defense. It's the exploitation of another species for your own benefit. My people decided a long time ago that that was unacceptable - even in the name of scientific progress.
- Kathryn Janeway, *Star Trek: Voyager*, "Scientific Method," 29 October 1997.

MacDonald quote / 72

For to such a pass has the worship of Knowledge...arrived, that its priests, men kind as other men to their children...will yet, in the worship of this their idol, in their greed after the hidden things of the life of the flesh, without scruple ...subject innocent, helpless, appealing, dumb souls to such tortures whose bare description would justly set me forth to the blame of cruelty toward those who sat listening to the same.
- George MacDonald, *Paul Faber, Surgeon*, 176.

for nothing / 73

"With the smaller ones, what we saw was that whenever we starved them, that there was a high rate of cannibalism."
- Cristina Richardson, former graduate student in the Department of Biology at the University of Alabama, in an interview with Bob McDonald, *Quirks & Quarks*, CBC Radio, 4 June 2011. This is her explanation for the purpose of the study, from the same interview:

"We want to produce them in a large quantity and keep our feed costs down to make it economical. So whenever you pack them too much and don't feed them enough, you have this issue of cannibalism....If you're trying to make a profit...you have to decide what amount of cannibalism is allowable."

Starving sea urchins. This may seem an odd example, when there are so many more obvious horrors taking place in laboratories all over the world. Hardly the same order of magnitude as Pavlov's dogs, dying in convulsions after their skulls were broken open with hammer, chisel, saw and drill (George Bernard Shaw, *Shaw on Vivisection* [London: Allen & Unwin, 1949], 15-17). But urchin or dog, starving or convulsing, torture is torture and a stolen life is a stolen life. This young scientist's detached description of deliberately starved sea urchins being driven to cannibalism is the particular grief I woke up to that morning.

the camel / 74

A photograph, spread over both pages, stark colours, a crowd of nameless faces blurring into the background as the one non-human being came into focus, and stopped my breath.

Reflection on a photograph by Alexandre Meneghini (Associated Press), "LightBox," *Time*, 17 October 2011, 12-13. Caption: "Tripoli residents converge around a camel set to be slaughtered in honor of Libyan rebels who died in the struggle against now ousted tyrant Muammar Gaddafi."

the end of words / 75

And that makes my words a blasphemy, because they are not for you.

Reflection on a photograph by Brent Stirton (Getty Images), in "Rhino Wars," by Peter Gwin, *National Geographic*, March 2012, 106-107. Caption: "Game Scouts found this black rhino bull wandering Zimbabwe's Savé Valley Conservancy after poachers shot it several times and hacked off both its horns. Veterinarians had to euthanize the animal because its shattered shoulder couldn't support its weight."

Other Voices

Buddha quote / 79

> *All tremble at violence;*
> *All fear death.*
> *Seeing others as like yourself,*
> *Do not kill or cause others to kill.*
>
> *All tremble at violence;*
> *Life is dear for all.*
> *Seeing others as like yourself,*
> *Do not kill or cause others to kill.*
>   - Buddha (c. 563-483 BCE), *Dhammapada* 129-130.

I begin *Other Voices* with Gautama Buddha's exhortation: "See yourself in others." This one theme reverberates throughout all the major religious traditions of the world, a rule so treasured that it is referred to as "Golden."

Buddhism: Treat not others in ways that you yourself would find hurtful.

Hinduism: Do not do to others what would cause pain if done to you.

Judaism: What is hateful to you, do not do to your neighbour.

Christianity: Do unto others as you would have others do unto you.

Islam: Wish for others what you wish for yourself.

Baha'i Faith: Lay not on anyone a load you would not wish laid upon you.

Jainism: Treat all creatures in the world as one would like to be treated.

This delicate thread of deepest wisdom weaves its unifying way across every cultural and religious divide, from ancient times to the present: recognize our kindredness, and we will be moved to kindness.

On the Eating of Flesh / 80

Plutarch (c. 45-120 CE), selected passages from "On the Eating of Flesh I," *Moralia*, Loeb Classical Library (1957), Vol. XII, 541-559.

"The tame goose and the dove within the household," as Sophocles says, were torn limb from limb and carved up for food; and men did not do this under the compulsion of hunger, as cats and weasels do, but simply for the pleasure of an appetizing taste. And so what is brutish and bloodthirsty in human nature was reinforced and made insensitive to pity, while the elements of kindness and gentleness lost most of their keenness. Acting on the contrary principle, the Pythagoreans, in order to promote loving kindness and compassion among men, were particularly careful to be kind to animals. For consistent regular behaviour is extraordinarily powerful, gradually infiltrating into the emotions and making men better.
- Plutarch, Moral Essays, trans. Rex Warner (Harmondsworth: Penguin, 1971), 99-100.

A Dog's Tale / 82

Mark Twain, "A Dog's Tale," in *The Birds and Beasts of Mark Twain*, ed. Robert M. Rodney and Minnie M. Brashear (Oklahoma: University of Oklahoma Press, 1966), 93-106. Abridged, sequence slightly altered.

Walker quote / 84

The animals of the world exist for their own reasons. They were not made for humans any more than black people were made for whites or women for men. This is the gist of Ms Spiegel's cogent, humane and astute argument, and it is sound.
- Alice Walker, foreword to *The Dreaded Comparison: Human and Animal Slavery*, by Marjorie Spiegel (New York: Mirror Books, 1996), 14.

wherever a heart beats / 85

James Oliver Curwood, preface to *Barry, Son of Kazan* (New York: Doubleday, Page & Company, 1925), vi-vii.

Grant quote / 86

George Grant, *Technology and Justice* (Toronto: Anansi, 1986), 55.

Bruno: A New Perspective on Happy Cows / 87

Alisa (Meadow) Rutherford-Fortunati, veganic grower and educator for Gentle World. Abridged and used by permission.

> *There is only one picture of Bruno because he always tried to lick me when I got too close...*
> - Meadow, email to the editor, 21 January 2013.

> *Man is the only animal that can remain on friendly terms with the victims he intends to eat until he eats them.*
> - Samuel Butler, *The Note-Books of Samuel Butler* (London: Chiswick Press, 1926), 78.

Buber quote / 90

Martin Buber, *I and Thou,* trans. Ronald Gregor Smith (Edinburgh: T. & T. Clark, 1937), 96.

In his seminal work *I and Thou,* Jewish philosopher Martin Buber distinguishes between the two basic attitudes we adopt in relation to others: I-It and I-Thou. If only we would look deeply enough into the eloquent eyes of animals, we would become to each other *I* and *Thou,* enriching our lives and saving theirs.

On a Mother's Love / 91

Holly Cheever, DVM, founding member of the Leadership Council of the Humane Society Veterinary Medical Association, and vice president of the New York State Humane Association. Originally published in *Times Union*, 23 August 2010. Used by permission.

> *My perspective of veganism was most affected by learning that the veal calf is a by-product of dairying, and that in essence there is a slice of veal in every glass of what I had thought was an innocuous white liquid - milk.*
> - Rynn Berry, quoted in *The Vegan Sourcebook*, by Joanne Stepaniak (Lincolnwood, IL: Lowell House, 2000), 40.

Jesus quote / 92

> *The Spirit of the Lord is on me,*
> *because he has anointed me*
> *to preach good news to the poor.*
> *He has sent me to proclaim*
> *freedom for the prisoners*
> *and recovery of sight for the blind,*
> *to release the oppressed...*
> - Jesus, Luke 4:18.

22815 / 93

Nathan Runkle, founder and executive director of Mercy For Animals. Adapted from a Mercy For Animals email bulletin, 18 December 2012. Used by permission.

Jane - one tiny chicken foot. . . / 94

Twyla Francois, director of investigations for Mercy For Animals Canada. Originally published by *United Poultry Concerns*, 12 December 2006. Used by permission.

My Life as an Undercover Investigator / 96

Cody Carlson, former undercover investigator for Mercy For Animals. Originally published in *VegNews*, 28 June 2012. Abridged and used by permission.

Tolstoy quote / 98

"A man can live and be healthy without killing animals for food; therefore, if he eats meat, he participates in taking animal life merely for the sake of his appetite. And to act so is immoral." It is so simple and indubitable that it is impossible not to agree with it. But because most people do eat meat, people, on hearing the case stated, admit its justice, and then, laughing, say; "But a good beefsteak is a good thing all the same; and I shall eat one at dinner today with pleasure."

- Leo Tolstoy, "Letter to Dr. Eugen Heinrich Schmitt," in Tolstoy's Writings on Civil Disobedience and Non-Violence (London: Peter Owen, 1967), 170-171.

its little tail / 99

Afterwards I went into the compartment where small animals are slaughtered – a very large chamber with asphalt floor, and tables with backs, on which sheep and calves are killed. Here the work was already finished; in the long room, impregnated with the smell of blood, were only two butchers. One was blowing into the leg of a dead lamb and patting the swollen stomach with his hand; the other, a young fellow in an apron besmeared with blood, was smoking a bent cigarette. There was no one else in the long dark chamber, filled with a heavy smell. After me there entered a man, apparently an ex-soldier, bringing in a young yearling ram, black with a white mark on its neck, and its legs tied. This animal he placed upon one of the tables, as if upon a bed. The old soldier greeted the butchers, with whom he was evidently acquainted, and began to ask when their master allowed them leave. The fellow with the cigarette approached with a knife, sharpened it on the edge of the table, and answered that they were free on holidays. The live ram was lying as quietly as the dead inflated one, except that it was briskly wagging its short little tail and its sides were heaving more quickly than usual. The soldier pressed down its uplifted head gently, without effort; the butcher, still continuing the conversation, grasped with his left hand the head of the ram and cut its throat. The ram quivered, and the little tail stiffened and ceased to wave. The fellow, while waiting for the blood to flow, began to relight his cigarette, which had gone out. The blood flowed and the ram began to writhe. The conversation continued without the

slightest interruption. It was horribly revolting....We cannot pretend that we do not know this. We are not ostriches, and cannot believe that if we refuse to look at what we do not wish to see, it will not exist. This is especially the case when what we do not wish to see is what we wish to eat.
   - Leo Tolstoy, *Essays and Letters*, 89-90.

Ashes

I began this book with an *Apologia* for empathy, then traced the roots of empathy in my life by *Looking Back* through the years leading up to my *Awakening*. Fully awake, I had no choice but to bear *Witness*, until finally coming to the end of my own words. This was followed by a collection of personal accounts written by *Other Voices* committed to speaking the truth.

My remaining reflections are marked by the residue of holocaust, by that which remains after the fires of grief and rage have burned themselves out. *Ashes*. They speak of mourning, of a world made greyer and darker by the knowledge of cruelty, suffering and death, of ashes to ashes and dust to dust. They speak of sorrow and wrongdoing, of complicity and confession, of longing to make restitution. Of foreheads smeared with awareness, and with hope.

Ashes, dark reminders of what has been, dormant promises of what can be.

ashes / 103

Every taste of the world is bitter now, ashen.

French filmmaker Georges Franju experienced this. After witnessing the slaughter of animals for his 1949 documentary *Le Sang des bêtes* (*The Blood of Animals*), he wrote:

> *Quand je suis allé la première fois là-dedans, je suis rentré chez moi, j'ai pleuré pendant deux jours, j'ai caché les couteaux, j'avais envie de mourir.* [The first time I went there, I returned home, I cried for two days, I hid the knives, I wanted to die.]
>   - *Georges Franju, cinéaste* (Paris: Maison de la Villette, 1992), 21.

If witnessing the inside of a slaughterhouse for just one day could have this impact on a mere observer, what happens to those who work there? Day after day, year after year, killing over and over and over again? Forcing the march towards death, overpowering gentle creatures as they struggle and plead to live, listening to screams of pain and terror, wielding instruments of death and dismemberment, being the last sight of another living being and then wading through her blood. Hardening oneself against it all.

What does it do to the human spirit to make a living brutalizing the meek and defenceless? What are we doing to those who do the killing for us?

Deliberate and egregious cruelty may not be standard practice, but it is rampant in factory farms and slaughterhouses. Whether these places breed sadism, or whether they merely provide concealed opportunities for its perpetration, those whose food choices demand the slaughter of animals are responsible not only for the suffering involved in sanctioned methods of killing, but also for the vicious beatings, the laughter at writhing bodies, and the coldly calculated maximization of suffering.

What could possibly motivate such violent hatred against captive creatures who are about to die? All I can think of is that these horrific acts of cruelty must be linked to unbearable guilt, with rage directed at helpless victims for being the cause of it. What other explanation can there be for this killer's response to suffering eyes accusing him:

You're already going to kill the hog, but that's not enough. It has to suffer....You go in hard, push hard, blow the windpipe, make it drown in its own blood. Split its nose. A live hog would be running around the pit. It would just be looking up at me and I'd be sticking, and I would just take my knife and - eerk - cut its eye out while it was just sitting there. And this hog would just scream.

One time I took my knife - it's sharp enough - and I sliced off the end of a hog's nose, just like a piece of bologna. The hog went crazy for a few seconds. Then it just sat there looking kind of stupid. So I took a handful of salt brine and ground it into his nose. Now that hog really went nuts, pushing its nose all over the place....I wasn't the only guy doing this kind of stuff....One guy I work with actually chases hogs into the scalding tank. And everybody - hog drivers, shacklers, utility men - uses lead pipes on hogs. Everybody knows it, all of it.

- Slaughterhouse worker Donny Tice (pseudonym), interviewed in Slaughterhouse: The Shocking Story of Greed, Neglect, and Inhumane Treatment Inside the U.S.

Meat Industry, by Gail Eisnitz (Amherst, NY: Prometheus Books, 2006), 92-94.

Gail Eisnitz, chief investigator for the Humane Farming Association (HFA), spent ten years doing the research for *Slaughterhouse*. It began with a letter that came to her from a slaughterhouse worker, claiming that cows were being skinned alive while fully conscious. Eisnitz confesses in her book that the slaughterhouse investigations nearly killed her.

thanksgiving / 104

I'm so bloody sorry.

Over and over again I experienced the words "I'm sorry" exploding onto the pages of my reflections. I removed the words later, recognizing in them a descent into self-pity, useless to those who have suffered and died. I leave these words here as witness to my shame, and my truth.

the cemetery / 105

Look behind you – hope is more real than the grave.

Grieving the death of Jesus, Mary bent over to look into his tomb. The story tells of two angels sitting there. Looking past her, they asked why she was crying; she turned to see what they were looking at, and saw Jesus standing there (interpretation of John 20:11-14).

This is what hope looks like to me, a conscious and deliberate turning away from death towards life, from despair towards love. Whether or not there is eternal hope for all living beings, as theologian George MacDonald believed (*The Hope of the Gospel*, 1892), there is no hope which is not at its heart a turn towards love and "reverence for life" (Schweitzer).

to be a life / 106

My child is lying on my knees;
The signs of Heaven she reads:
My face is all the Heaven she sees,
Is all the Heaven she needs.

And she is well, yea bathed in bliss,
If Heaven lies in my face;
Behind it all is tenderness
And truthfulness and grace....

If I, so often full of doubt,
So true to her can be,
Thou who dost see all round about,
Art very true to me.

If I am low and sinful, bring
More love where need is rife;
Thou knowest what an awful thing
It is to be a Life...

    - George MacDonald, "A Mother's Hymn," in *George MacDonald and His Wife*, by Greville MacDonald (London: George Allen & Unwin, 1924), 199-200.

Let me learn by paradox
that the way down is the way up,
that to be low is to be high,
that the broken heart is the healed heart...

    - "Introductory: The Valley of Vision," in *The Valley of Vision: A Collection of Puritan Prayers & Devotions*, ed. Arthur Bennett (Edinburgh: The Banner of Truth Trust, 1975), xv.

playing god / 107

...I had woken up to a news item about pigs....Genetically modified, unwanted, killed.

The University of Guelph, which holds the patent for the so-called Enviropigs, quietly killed the remaining animals last month....Calling the deaths a "sad but necessary conclusion to an unwanted and unnecessary GE experiment," Lucy Sharratt of the Canadian Biotechnology Action Network said the regulatory review process should be aborted immediately because there is no longer the scientific capacity at the University of Guelph to answer any questions arising from Health Canada's ongoing safety assessment of Enviropigs for human food and animal feed....

The pigs were euthanized on May 24...just days after North America's largest farm animal protection group launched a public campaign to save the lives of the swine. New York-based Farm Sanctuary offered to work with the university to find "loving homes for the Enviropigs" to "live out their unnatural lives as naturally as possible."

Bona Hunt said that the university received "many generous and well-intentioned offers," but there was "absolutely no opportunity for this to occur, as adoption, donation or transfer of the animals would represent a breach of protocols and Canadian policies."

- Sarah Schmidt, "Genetically engineered pigs killed after funding ends," *Postmedia News*, 22 June 2012.

What do we do with the billions of lives that we create only to destroy?

Have they no rights in this their compelled existence?
- George MacDonald, *Paul Faber, Surgeon*, 176.

"Hateful day when I received life!...Cursed creator!"
- Mary Wollstonecraft Shelley, *Frankenstein; or, The Modern Prometheus*, 2nd ed. (New York: Longman, 2007), 99.

Singer quote / 108

Isaac Bashevis Singer, foreword to *Vegetarianism: A Way of Life,* by Dudley Giehl (New York: Harper & Row, 1979), ix.

at the gate / 109

Your name is easy on their lips, but their garments are stained with blood.

How is it possible to look for God and sing his praises while insulting and degrading his creatures? If, as I had thought, all lambs are the Agnus Dei [Lamb of God], then to deprive them of light and the field and their joyous frisking and the sky is the worst kind of blasphemy.
- Malcolm Muggeridge, quoted in "Fear Factories: The case for compassionate conservatism – for animals," by Matthew Scully, *The American Conservative*, 23 May 2005, 13.

They stand at your gate with the screams of their victims ringing in your ears.

The Lord said, "What have you done? Listen! Your brother's
blood cries out to me from the ground."
　- Genesis 4:10.

The author of the biblical book of Genesis portrayed the blood of Abel as crying out to God against his brother and murderer, Cain. Yet the story passes over the blood of Abel's victim, the firstborn lamb he had killed, allowing it to seep into the ground in silence, its apparent insignificance reverberating through thousands of years of sacrificial massacre. The ancient texts say nothing of the victims' cries and screams and bellows of fear and pain, but commend the stench of burning flesh as "an aroma pleasing to the Lord" (Leviticus 1:17).

And yet even there, in the midst of that brutal ancient world with its desperate clawing at survival, a small mercy peeks out like a pathetic orphan from texts filled with rituals of slaughter: "Do not cook a young goat in its mother's milk" (Exodus 23:19). I think of that small lost mercy as I see affluent people today gorging themselves on unnecessary suffering, thoughtlessly mixing meat and dairy, not thinking of the fact that they are consuming the body parts of babies covered in the milk their mothers made for suckling them.

How dare they stand at the gates of Love with a knife in their hands?

To this day there are those who would rather twist their moral sensibilities into intricate contortions than risk the collapse of their dependence on an infallible biblical record. Yet even within the Bible itself, we find that later writers were not afraid to look back on earlier texts with a critical eye, unwilling to accept depictions of God that were incompatible with the central scriptural revelation of divine justice and love:

> *I have no pleasure in the blood of bulls and lambs and goats.*
> *When you come to meet with me, who has asked this of you...?*
> *Stop bringing meaningless offerings!...Your hands are full of*
> *blood; wash and make yourselves clean. Take your evil deeds*
> *out of my sight! Stop doing wrong, learn to do right! Seek*
> *justice, encourage the oppressed.*
> 　- Isaiah 1:11-13, 15-17.

> *I desire mercy, not sacrifice, and acknowledgment of God*
> *rather than burnt offerings.*
> 　- Hosea 6:6.

If you had known what these words mean, "I desire mercy, not sacrifice," you would not have condemned the innocent.
- Jesus, Matthew 12:7.

Feed my lambs....Take care of my sheep....Feed my sheep.
- Jesus, John 21:15-17.

arches / 110

Arcs of trajectory for thoughts that have nowhere to go...

Some things have not changed since I wrote this reflection. Arches of trees reaching over the road towards my home, arches of faith-longing in ancient European cathedrals, and arches of cold profit feeding mass cruelty to unsuspecting children.

But my words no longer form an arc over my own head, returning again and again to injure me. I am sending them out into the world now, for wounding and for healing. They bear my hopes for a more merciful future, where "grief will turn to joy" (John 16:20).

St. Paul quote / 112

Rejoice with those who rejoice, weep with those who weep.
- Romans 12:15 New Revised Standard Version.

peripheral vision / 113

Suffering Love at the heart of this broken universe.

The God of the whole Bible is a suffering God. God suffers because God loves. And until that which God loves - the creation - is healed, the glory of God can only be glimpsed by those who in some measure are given to participate in God's suffering love.
- Douglas John Hall, *Professing the Faith: Christian Theology in a North American Context* (Minneapolis: Fortress Press, 1993), 183.

Coetzee and Singer quotes / 114

In Germany, we say, a certain line was crossed which took people beyond the ordinary murderousness and cruelty of warfare into a state that we can only call sin....A sickness of the soul continued to mark that generation. It marked those citizens of the Reich who had committed evil actions, but also those who, for whatever reason, were in ignorance of those actions. It thus marked, for practical purposes, every citizen of the Reich. Only those in the camps were innocent....Let me say it openly: we are surrounded by an enterprise of degradation, cruelty, and killing which rivals anything that the Third Reich was capable of, indeed dwarfs it, in that ours is an enterprise without end, self-regenerating, bringing rabbits, rats, poultry, livestock ceaselessly into the world for the purpose of killing them.

- J. M. Coetzee, *The Lives of Animals*, 20-21.

A single mouse had found its way into the apartment, and every night Herman set out for her a piece of bread, a small slice of cheese, and a saucer of water to keep her from eating the books....Occasionally, she would venture out of her hole even when the light was on. Herman had even given her a Hebrew name: Huldah. Her little bubble eyes stared at him with curiosity. She stopped being afraid of him....What had become of Huldah? How awful that throughout his long illness he had entirely forgotten her. No one had fed her or given her anything to drink. "She is surely dead," he said to himself. "Dead of hunger and thirst!"...Despair took hold of Herman....In his thoughts, Herman spoke a eulogy for the mouse who had shared a portion of her life with him and who, because of him, had left this earth. "What do they know - all those scholars, all those philosophers, all the leaders of the world - about such as you? They have convinced themselves that man, the worst transgressor of all the species, is the crown of creation. All other creatures were created merely to provide him with food, pelts, to be tormented, exterminated. In relation to them, all people are Nazis, for the animals it is an eternal Treblinka. And yet man demands compassion from heaven." Herman clapped his hands to his mouth. "I mustn't live, I mustn't! I can no longer be a part of it!"...He heard a slight noise that sounded like a child sucking. Herman sat up and saw Huldah. She appeared thinner, weak, and her fur looked grayer, as if she had aged....Herman was not a man who wept....But now his face became wet and hot. It wasn't fated

that he bear the guilt of a murderer. Providence - aware of every molecule, every mite, every speck of dust - had seen to it that the mouse received its nourishment during his long sleep.
- Isaac Bashevis Singer, "The Letter Writer," in *Collected Stories: Gimpel the Fool to The Letter Writer* (New York: Library of America, 2004), 724-755. (Reference to "eternal Treblinka" found on p. 750.)

holocaust / 115

I sat in the movie theatre...

It was the 1960s, I was a child, alone at the movie theatre. A short newsreel preceded the feature film. Piles and piles of starved and naked human bodies at a concentration camp. It was a defining moment of my childhood, awakening me to the existence of evil and suffering in the world. My life has been indelibly marked by what I saw that day.

I sit now watching again...

Slaughterhouse videos do not expose static evidence of past atrocities. They record the torture in the process of its infliction, the terror as it is being experienced, the screams as they are uttered, the bodies in their writhing, the blows as they are falling, the blood spurting.

There is too much evidence – we can't say that we do not know.

I am not equating the Holocaust with the millions of animals slaughtered every week for US dinner tables, for we differ in many ways. Yet, we all share a love of life and our ability to experience many emotions, including affection, joy, sadness, and fear.

I do see a striking parallel in the mindsets of both sets of oppressors: their self-image as upstanding members of their communities, their abject objectification of their victims, their callous use of cattle cars for transport, their continuous refinement of killing line technology, their preoccupation with record keeping and cost-effectiveness, their eagerness to hide and masquerade their horrendous deeds.
- Alex Hershaft, holocaust survivor and founder of Farm Animal Rights Movement (FARM), quoted in "Holocaust survivor fights to save 'The Walking Dead' – Slaughterhouse Animals," by Julie Hanan, *Examiner*, 14 October 2012.

From my point of view, the ongoing holocaust of animals is as terrible and horrific as the Holocaust of people. Both were perpetrated on living creatures. The one group suffered and the other group continues to suffer. Then the world declined to intervene and now the world declines to intervene.

In my eyes, there is no difference between one kind of suffering and another. The only difference is that the holocaust of the animals can be stopped....I still can't comprehend how an enlightened person is capable of ignoring the scandalous gap that exists between the amount of suffering caused to animals when they are being murdered, and the amount of pleasure such an enlightened person gets from eating their flesh.

- Eyal Megged, "Stop the animal holocaust," *Haaretz*, 7 September 2012.

Is there any reason why we should be suffered to torment them? Not any that I can see. Are there any why we should not be suffered to torment them? Yes...the question is not, Can they reason? nor, Can they talk? but, Can they suffer?

- Jeremy Bentham, *An Introduction to the Principles of Morals and Legislation*, 82-83n.

as they see us / 116

...we tear them apart...

As I witness deliberate cruelties inflicted on helpless and innocent creatures, as my body trembles with grief and rage, it is hatred that I find rising up inside of me. Hatred, the root of violence, is in me too. It rises like bile in my throat, choking and poisoning the love out of me. I know that the only way to turn this world towards mercy is through love and not through hate, but how can I hold on to love in the face of what I have seen?

I look to these gentle creatures and see in them a purity of heart surpassing our own. If only we would share life with them, cease our warfare against them, humble ourselves before them, we would receive something immeasurably more important than everything we are presently stealing from them.

Later, when Ged thought back upon that night, he knew that had none touched him when he lay thus spirit-lost, had none called him back in some way, he might have been lost for good. It was only the dumb instinctive wisdom of the beast who licks his hurt companion to comfort him, and yet in that wisdom Ged saw something akin to his own power....From that time forth he believed that the wise man is one who never sets himself apart from other living things, whether they have speech or not, and in later years he strove long to learn what can be learned, in silence, from the eyes of animals...
- Ursula LeGuin, *A Wizard of Earthsea* (Harmondsworth: Puffin Books, 1968), 96-97.

shalom / 117

Why is it we who are seen as ill?

Hearts that are well do what hearts do when faced with the suffering of others – they break. By observers, and even by the one experiencing the grief, this may be perceived as a kind of sickness. But in reality it is the only healthy response.

With an unresting, vital force, reverence for life works upon the mind it has entered and throws it into the disquietude of a responsibility which never ceases.
- Albert Schweitzer, *The Animal World of Albert Schweitzer*, 170.

...our lives a unity of love...

I cannot do otherwise than cling to the fact that in me the will-to-live strives to be one with other wills-to-live. That is the light that shines in my darkness....When I rescue an insect from the puddle, then life has given itself to life, and the division of life within itself has ceased. When my life devotes itself to another life in any way whatever, my finite will-to-live communes with the infinite will in which all life is one. I find refreshment which keeps me from dying of thirst in the desert of life.
- Albert Schweitzer, *The Animal World of Albert Schweitzer*, 171.

...working for the shalom of this earth.

Shalom, the Hebrew word for peace. Not simply the absence of conflict, rather a peace that refuses to be confined within words or concepts. Wholeness, wellness, unity, harmony, happiness, every nuance of what "peace" can possibly signify, pushed beyond the boundaries of definition and finding its way, ultimately, into silent longings and prophetic imaginings. We may never reach that idyllic future when "kindness and truth meet together" and where "justice and peace kiss each other" (Psalm 85:10), but the vision of *shalom* shows us the direction, empowers the journey, and leaves no one behind as we move towards wellness for all.

Herbert quote / 118

With sick and famisht eyes,
With doubling knees and weary bones,
To thee my cries,
To thee my grones,
To thee my sighs, my tears ascend:
No end?
My throat, my soul is hoarse;
My heart is wither'd...
- George Herbert, "Longing," *The Temple*, 1633.

weary / 119

When the grief eases and the rage subsides, it is weariness I am left with. Each phase has its individual temptations, and its particular possibilities. Weariness weakens us and tempts us to despair, but it also carries with it a unique potential for determined faithfulness in the face of apparent futility. It is in acts of faithfulness that hope is revived.

> *All the good we may recognize or desire is nothing in itself and leads nowhere unless it is strengthened in the thought of faithfulness. It is just like the hardening of metal. No one can explain how it happens. First it is weak and pliable, but then it becomes a hundred times as strong as it was before. Nor can we explain how every human virtue only achieves strength and fulfillment after it has been hardened on the anvil of faithfulness.*
> - Albert Schweitzer, *The Words of Albert Schweitzer*, 49.

Parting Words

In Carol Shields' novel *Unless*, a young woman breaks after witnessing a traumatic event. Norah's friends and family look on helplessly as she descends into silence and incapacity. Day after day she sits on a street corner with a cardboard sign for passersby to read. On the sign she has written one word, in capital letters: **GOODNESS**.

Suffering Eyes is an account of my awakening to the traumatic events taking place in the lives of animals all around us, because of us. I have tried to bear witness, both to their suffering and to my complicity. I too have broken because of what I have seen. I have wrestled with words, conscripting them as best I can for the awakening of empathy and mercy, for the urgency of rescue. And where words fail, I imagine myself on some street corner holding my own cardboard sign in silence, with one word for passersby: **KINDNESS**.

Here I hold that word up, in grief and in hope.

I would not want to end this reminiscence with despair. Whenever I wrote a novel...they're always filled with sadness also, and despair. But I never published a novel if I don't have a way out. An appeal of hope and to hope, and for hope. I don't think that I survived, I don't think I have been given years, to give you despair....Hope is possible, simply because hope is necessary.
- Elie Wiesel, "An Evening with Elie Wiesel."

all I want / 123

My mother passed away in August 2012. During her final years, we shared many loving hours together. She longed for my happiness, just as I long for the happiness of those I love.

I just want you to be happy.
If we all said that, and if we meant it, as a mother would, for every one of this earth's little children, maybe I could taste a measure of what my mother wants for me.

Whitman quote / 187

Walt Whitman, "Shut not your doors," in *The Pocket Book of Modern Verse*, ed. Oscar Williams (New York: Washington Square Press, 1972), 4.

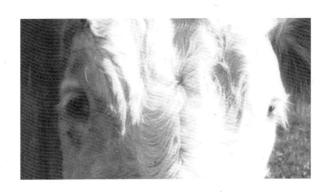

Afterword

Hope
Calvin Neufeld

Perhaps it is easy, after reading this, to despair – despair being consumption by grief. But that is not the intention of *Suffering Eyes*. This is a book about hope. It is a chronicle of awakening, and in awakening there is hope.

Elie Wiesel, in recounting his memories of the holocaust, offers "an appeal of hope and to hope, and for hope. I don't think that I survived, I don't think I have been given years, to give you despair....Hope is possible, simply because hope is necessary."

Yes, hope is necessary. But it's not its own goal, in itself it is nothing, empty. This book is not about having hope, it's about creating hope. What's important is awakening. Hope, then, is the consequence.

My mother chose to end her book with a single quote, a line from the poem "Shut not your doors" by Walt Whitman: "The words of my book nothing, the drift of it every thing."

After reading *Suffering Eyes*, it may be tempting to dwell on the stories and think "What do I do with my grief? How do I carry the memories of so much suffering?" It's the question Elizabeth Costello asks in her despair: "Calm down, I tell myself, you are making a mountain out of a molehill. This is life. Everyone else comes to terms with it, why can't you? *Why can't you?*"

Like Mary weeping at Jesus' grave, consumed by grief, my mother writes to herself, "Look behind you – hope is more real than the grave." Turn, turn from the grief. Why? What's behind you? Hope?

No, not hope, but life. Life goes on. It's life that matters. Grieve at death, yes, then turn. There is always more life, with all its solemn responsibility and desperate need and tenderness and truthfulness and grace, so, as the song says, "Turn! Turn! Turn!" But when you turn from grief, be sure that your eyes are wide open, that in your vision is included all life, none of it shut out of your consciousness. Shut not your eyes. Awaken. *See* the life in your garden, the life in your home, the life everywhere. That seeing is compassion.

Compassion is total, it is a relationship with life. Compassion that has limits, or compassion that is selective, is not compassion, it's just an abstraction. The real thing is total, a simple relationship with everything that lives: "your suffering is my suffering, your peace, my peace." Compassion is not a *command* to "do unto others as you would have them do unto you." Compassion is the *inability* to do to others as you would not have done to you because your pain is my pain because *I see you*.

Suffering Eyes is not an appeal to hope, it is an appeal to awakening that relationship with life. Hope is simply the consequence.

The words of my book nothing, the drift of it every thing.

Walt Whitman